The
Green
Witch's
Grimoire

The Green Witch's *Grimoire*

Your Complete Guide to CREATING YOUR OWN BOOK OF NATURAL MAGIC

ARIN MURPHY-HISCOCK
Author of *The Green Witch*

Adams Media
New York London Toronto Sydney New Delhi

Aadamsmedia

Adams Media
An Imprint of Simon & Schuster, Inc.
100 Technology Center Drive
Stoughton, MA 02072

First Adams Media hardcover edition July 2020

ADAMS MEDIA and colophon are trademarks of Simon & Schuster.

For information about special discounts for bulk purchases, please contact Simon & Schuster Special Sales at 1-866-506-1949 or business@simonandschuster.com.

The Simon & Schuster Speakers Bureau can bring authors to your live event. For more information or to book an event contact the Simon & Schuster Speakers Bureau at 1-866-248-3049 or visit our website at www.simonspeakers.com.

Interior design by Priscilla Yuen
Interior images © Simon & Schuster, Inc.; 123RF/jakkapan jabjainai, Marina Vorontsova; Getty Images/Nata_Slavetskaya, kenny371

Manufactured in the United States of America

5 2022

Library of Congress Cataloging-in-Publication Data
Names: Murphy-Hiscock, Arin, author.
Title: The green witch's grimoire / Arin Murphy-Hiscock, author of The Green Witch.
Description: First Adams Media hardcover edition July 2020. | Avon, Massachusetts: Adams Media, 2020.
Series: Green witch. | Includes bibliographical references and index.
Identifiers: LCCN 2020014947 | ISBN 9781507213544 (hc) | ISBN 9781507213551 (ebook)
Subjects: LCSH: Grimoires. | Witchcraft. | Magic.
Classification: LCC BF1558 .M86 2020 | DDC 133.4/3--dc23
LC record available at https://lccn.loc.gov/2020014947

ISBN 978-1-5072-1354-4
ISBN 978-1-5072-1355-1 (ebook)

Contents

PART 2
Using Your Green Witch Grimoire / 109

Introduction

*A grimoire is an organic, evolving piece
of art and magic.*

It is a record of magic, spells, and rituals, and also a reflection of your spirit. Your grimoire serves as a record of your work, a journal chronicling your development, a place to note down interesting bits of knowledge, a resource for information, and a collection of your learning and ongoing education—it's a manual, a dictionary, and a collection of inspiring ideas all in one. It is both an inspiration and a tool.

The Green Witch's Grimoire will help you create your own grimoire, where you can record information like moon phases, seasonal information, and also spells, rituals, observations, and other practices to help you keep a history of your practice of green witchcraft. A grimoire is especially important for the green witch because unlike many other paths, the path of the green witch rests on your philosophy of living and how you interact with the world around you. For this reason, your prayers, rituals, and spells must be personally meaningful, and creating a record of this personal practice is key to living a fulfilling life as a green witch.

Creating a physical grimoire is an act of love and reverence for yourself, for the natural world around you, and for your path. It will deepen your understanding of how your practice evolves, and how you yourself develop and grow spiritually. Using this book as your guide, you will create your ideal grimoire. The first part of this book will help you create and craft your grimoire, from deciding on your paper and ink colors to organizing your content. The second part will then guide you through using your newly created grimoire in your green witch practice.

Your grimoire will be a balance between something beautiful and something practical. Grow your grimoire from the ground up with this guide, and learn how to use it to support your spiritual journey as a green witch.

NOTE This book is aimed at green witches who have some grounding in energy work and spiritual practice. As such, we won't be going over how to do basic rites or spells. Instead, I'll refer you to *The Green Witch* to learn about or refresh your familiarity with general practices.

How to Use This Book

Building a grimoire is a valuable practice that can enhance your understanding of your personal practice and development. It reflects your choices from the ground up, from vague concept to physical collection of information and records.

This book is not a grimoire itself. It has some information you can transcribe into your own grimoire but it doesn't function as a grimoire. Instead, it's a how-to, a guide to outlining and planning your own collection of knowledge and reference.

There's nothing wrong with consulting existing collections of spells and rituals, whether they're published or privately assembled. Seeing how other people have chosen to organize their books can be eye-opening and offer you a different way of looking at how you record information. In the end, however, in order for your spiritual practice to gain the full benefit from your grimoire, it should be as personal as possible.

Your grimoire can and will become a magical tool in its own right. It can't help but become one, through your repeated use and interfacing with it. It will absorb the energy you invest in it, and its contents will trace your spiritual development and experiences. To enable this, however, you have to take it seriously and devote time to it. Make it a regular practice to sit down after a spell, ritual, or meditation session and record specifics as well as your feelings about it. Record your experiences participating in other people's rituals, or following someone else's guided meditation. Be aware that you are crafting a magical tool.

In the end, as reassuring as a book full of someone else's rituals, spells, and correspondence lists can be, your own collection will be much more powerful and useful to you. Give your grimoire the focus and attention it deserves, and you'll discover that your practice can offer you so much more than you might have initially expected.

PART 1

Designing Your Green Witch Grimoire

THERE IS A LOT TO THINK ABOUT BEFORE you plunge into starting a grimoire. While you could go where your whims take you, you might run into problems later on if the way you've started doesn't work easily with how you want to include things, add information, or use the grimoire in practical or magical ways.

Take the time to really plan your grimoire out. How will you use it? What will be easiest for you? What might be more challenging but yield more benefit along the way? Do you want to leave options open for alternate or supportive uses down the road? What about developing a system that allows for expansion later on?

Green witchcraft is about the development of the self in tandem with the energy of nature; it is a development that is always in motion. In other words, the journey is the point, not the destination. Take that into account and enjoy the process of designing your grimoire from the ground up.

CHAPTER 1

What Is a Grimoire?

THE PRACTICE OF THE GREEN WITCH doesn't have a lot of bells and whistles, fancy tools, or complicated rituals. Perhaps more than any other path of witchcraft, the path of the green witch rests on your philosophy of living and how you interact with the world around you. For this reason, your prayers, the rituals you perform, and your sacred space must be personally meaningful. Creating a personal practice that accurately reflects who you are and your desire to work to create harmony in the world around you is the key to living a satisfying and fulfilling life as a green witch. To aid and support you along this path is a tool that may not seem critical but can be your most valuable companion along the way—the grimoire.

The first step in any undertaking is gaining an understanding of the subject. This chapter will discuss what a grimoire is, the history of grimoires, and what a modern grimoire would look like. You'll also learn about a grimoire's uses, the various applications of a modern version, and the goals of creating one.

A Grimoire Is a Reflection of You

Popular entertainment presents a grimoire as a spell book, often with complicated diagrams and rituals. Sometimes a magic user is powerless without it. Sometimes an unsuspecting person ends up with the grimoire and accidentally casts one of the spells.

You already know that's not how magic works.

A grimoire is a record of magic, spells, rituals, and related information. It's an aggregate of your spiritual journey, a record of your growth and development. It's a collection of favorite rituals, prayers, invocations, inspirational quotations, and art.

A grimoire is a living, evolving piece of art and magic. It will never be complete or perfect. Your needs will change, and your grimoire will change to serve them. What results is a fascinating scrapbook of your evolution as a green witch. Ultimately, a modern grimoire is exactly what you want it to be. It can encompass as little or as much as you like.

HOW TO DEFINE YOUR GRIMOIRE

There are various iterations of grimoires that don't actually use the term. A grimoire can serve many purposes for different people:

- Some practitioners consider their grimoires to be a textbook from which to teach students. They're an educational tool, a collection of lessons and knowledge to pass on.

- Some people consider their grimoires to be a recipe book to consult. Their grimoires are an assortment of spells, rituals, and recorded recipes for incense, herbal teas, oils, and so forth.

- Others use their grimoires like a devotional book of hours— a collection of prayers, invocations, and affirmations for various situations or times of day or year.

All these things are important, and because green witchcraft isn't a traditional path, all these things can belong in your grimoire. (That doesn't necessarily mean physically in the same book, however. See Chapter 4 for a discussion of setting up the physical system for your grimoire.) A modern grimoire can be all these things and more. Trying to limit it can feel like trying to define the undefinable. In the end, your grimoire is what you need it to be.

You might be familiar with the term *Book of Shadows*. This is a Wicca-specific term for a grimoire that includes ritual texts, initiatory information, and Wicca-specific lore. It's a term that has trickled through to other magical paths, and so it's often used interchangeably with *grimoire*. You may also have seen the term *Mirror Book*, which is a modern term sometimes used to refer to a magical journal.

Grimoires Through History

Generally, when someone talks about a grimoire, they're thinking of one of the books collecting magical knowledge and details about talisman crafting, demon summoning and banishing, secret alphabets, and other occult practices that have come down through the Western mystery tradition. These tend to be associated with high, noble magic, as opposed to the low, common magic associated with wisewomen and hedge witches. (There was very definitely a class and gender division at work here, which is a discussion for another day. Suffice it to say that at this point of history, educated men were associated with intellectual magic that was heavy on ceremony, theory, and spiritual improvement, whereas uneducated women and men would participate in more practical magic associated with the household, healing, and family.)

It is important to remember that *grimoire* is a European term. Other cultures also have collections of spells, rituals, and magical knowledge, but the term *grimoire* is attributed to European works.

Grimoires began simply as quick-reference "grammar books" for sorcerers, magicians, and priests before evolving into comprehensive guides to magic, complete with spell-casting rituals, magical alphabets, and instructions to create amulets and talismans. With the advent of the printing press, some grimoires were mass-produced, but many of the abbreviations were misinterpreted and magical words misspelled, rendering them ineffective. The most powerful grimoires remained not only secret but also heavily encoded, making them accessible only to the highest initiates of the magical traditions.

There is value in studying grimoires that have survived history. However, these books aren't the kind of book you'll be creating. First of all, they were created by others, whose interests and goals were different from yours. Second, once the printing press came into use and people attempted to mass-produce grimoires, errors crept in accidentally to alter the information, and some errors were intentionally introduced in order to guard the secrets within the books. This ensured that the knowledge in them could be only theoretical.

What Does a Modern Grimoire Contain?

Everyone's grimoire will be different. Remember, your grimoire will reflect you, your interests, your areas of specialization, and your personal correspondences. In general, however, these are the kinds of things a green witch's grimoire might contain:

- **A dedication, blessing, manifesto, or mission statement.** This is the purpose of your grimoire and your work on the green witch path.

- **Information on your path, its tenets, and its rules or laws.** If you are a solitary practitioner, then you have the opportunity to define all of this. It can be a place to state your moral and ethical approach and express your feelings about your work as a green witch as it relates to the world at large.

- **Information on deities and spirits.** If there are deities or spirits that you find inspirational or work with, then information on them, their cultural significance, and myths or legends about them can be included.

- **Information on festivals and celebrations.** You can include information on the festivals and celebrations you wish to incorporate into your green witch practice, such as solstices and equinoxes, modern pagan festivals, or other cultural festivals. Writing texts for celebrating these things and including them in your grimoire is also a good idea. Using the same ritual for the same purpose regularly creates resonance within your practice and your spirit throughout time.

- **Correspondences.** Working with the natural world means being knowledgeable about supplies and materials. Keeping a reference of the correspondences of things like plants, stones, moon cycles, sun cycles, elements, tools, and symbols is one of the most important things you can do. Remember that correspondences aren't just magical; keep information about practical and medicinal uses as well. This is where to note down regularly occurring natural phenomena that could impact your work with energy, such as regular meteor showers, and planetary associations and energies.

- **Recipes and spells.** Another word for a collection of things like this is a *formulary*. Nearly every witch has some sort of formulary that is composed of a collection of recipes, spells, formulas, and guidelines for putting together various charms and items for a variety of purposes. Oil blends, incense blends, herbal combos, and teas for specific goals are all common in a section like this. Spells are another aspect of a formulary; you can record every spell you create, or record the ones you've tested and have decided to keep for future use. (Don't leave any spell completely unrecorded, however; see Chapter 7 for guidelines on recording spell successes, failures, and outcomes.)

- **Reflection.** Journaling and record-keeping are critical to your development as a green witch. Recording dreams, divinations, and other experiences will also contribute to your aggregate of lore that helps shape your development. Gratitude, meditation, and working out ideas are all essential to your development. Change is critical in all aspects of life, but especially so in the path of a green witch. A green witch works to change things for the better, to heal, and to support healthy growth. Being able to reflect on your practice and trace change is one of the things that enables you to gain a deeper understanding of how your spirituality unfolds and how to fine-tune your path ahead.

- **Inspiration.** You can use art, poetry, and snippets of text that evoke feelings in you—your grimoire is a place for these as well. Feeding the energy of your imagination is important; it allows for creativity to spark and build. Your grimoire doesn't have to be dry and serious; you can include joy and beauty also. Just make sure to note the origins of anything you copy into it to keep the source as clear as possible. Remember that what you include brings energy with it too.

The Three Functions of a Grimoire

Your grimoire is perhaps your most valuable resource as a green witch. It's a repository of information and inspiration that you can go to for insight into your practice, your relationship with the world around you, and your journey as a green witch. You can use it as an inspiration for new spells and rituals. If you have a question or an idea, your grimoire should be the first place you go to consult or expand on it. Your grimoire serves three specific functions: reference, record, and reflection.

REFERENCE

Perhaps most akin to the popular perception of the grimoire, a collection of reference information provides you with a distillation of your research about various topics that you feel is important enough to have at your fingertips for ease of consultation.

What you consider an important reference depends on your focus in your green witch practice. In my grimoire, I include subjects such as the following:

- Herb, tree, and flower references
- Planetary and other correspondences

- References for symbols, deities, and animal energies
- Records of spells, rituals, and meditations
- Planning work for rituals and spells
- Recipes and formulas

When I began practicing, I also included two other categories:

- Basic information regarding ritual
- Art and inspirational poetry or quotations

These latter subjects tapered off as I became more secure in my practice and in forging my own grimoire. At first I expected to use it as a go-to for ritual use, but in the long run, it has become more of a reference book for me. My personal grimoire also exists in the form of several separate books and binders; I'd need a small wagon to tote it around in its entirety. In general, I use a hardback notebook for journaling, planning, writing ideas, making notes as I read and research, recording responses to workings, and traveling. I have a binder for rituals as they are created, another for workshops I have developed (something else I journal, after every session), a separate herbal grimoire book with pressed samples or sketches accompanying information, and digital versions of many of these.

In other words, my resource is specific to me, and it reflects my interests, goals, and habits. Yours will (and should) look entirely different. You create this resource yourself by collecting experiences, lore, references, and other such data. You do this by creating a record as you practice.

Remember, your grimoire will evolve over time. That's a good thing. You may also phase out certain aspects of it as your practice evolves or add new sections as necessary.

RECORD

Recording covers two different kinds of information. The first is lore, knowledge, and research. As you progress, you'll be drawn or inspired to research various things—symbology, history, herbalism, cultures, specific religious practices from a certain era in a specific location—and as you read and research, you'll take notes and record specific bits of information you feel are valuable or pertinent. Your grimoire is the place to do that. Everyone begins by copying pretty rituals or invocations or spells from other books or practitioners who inspire them. There's a time and place for that, but it shouldn't form the majority of your grimoire.

The grimoire is also a record of your practice. Your grimoire should be a record of your own work, your experiments, and the results of your exercises. Looking at other people's work can enrich and inspire you, but your personal interactions with spirit and the natural world are what make your grimoire unique and yours. The value of your grimoire lies in what you bring to it, not what others do.

Over time, your grimoire will provide an overview of where you were spiritually, what you focused on, and how you grew and developed. Records are critical to your practice. Not only are they a way for you to keep track of the work you've done, but they also are a way for you to trace specific patterns in that work. Were there themes that surfaced over and over? Do works with certain ingredients fail consistently or turn out a little off from what you expected?

Finally, the act of recording makes you more aware. The act of observing and noting what you're doing and thinking reinforces your general awareness, both of the energy around you and your own. These kinds of things can be valuable insights.

Disciplined record-keeping is a skill, and one that isn't innate to most people. You do have to train yourself to do it, and it may be challenging at first. But stick with it; don't let it drop, even if it seems boring, useless, or unimportant. In the beginning, it will be awkward, and your collected records won't seem like they carry any sort of valuable information at all. The separate records aren't what is important. In time, the overall collection of records will take on its own energy and provide you with an overview of your work. Think of it like a lab report or a scientific experiment. A single record doesn't show you very much, because there isn't a larger body of information to compare it to in order to make connections and cross-references. But a year of experimentation and lab reports gives you a much better idea of what is going on, and is a richer aggregate of information.

The next function can't take place if the recording doesn't happen. Recording allows you the opportunity to reflect.

REFLECTION

The grimoire offers you the opportunity for reflection in two ways. The first is a reflection of your spirituality and your spiritual journey, engaging the grimoire's function as a physical record of your activity. The second is an opportunity to reflect on issues and ideas that mean a lot to you, exploring your response to them through magical journaling.

Magical journaling is an important activity. It isn't the same as recording a spell or adding notes about its effects that you notice a week or so later. Magical journaling covers your perception of the journey itself, as well as meditation and shamanic or spirit journeying. It's the part where you can wax philosophical, work out how you feel about aspects of your practice, brainstorm about concepts and ideas, and spill out emotional reactions to things. Writing is a form of magic, bringing thought into the physical world via the act of writing. The words you write and sentences you create resonate with your energy and ideas. Words have power, as most practitioners know, and yours are important to your spiritual practice. Working out ideas via words is a way to try to capture and define ideas, bringing the abstract into a more concrete form. For a more in-depth look at journaling, see Chapter 8.

From Brainstorming to Planning

Information, reference material, copies of spells and rituals, and records of workings and meditations: All these things make your personal grimoire what it is. In time, you'll have a better sense of what information you want to continue recording and what you no longer need to refer back to.

Having considered the uses of a grimoire and what kinds of information it can contain, you can now move on to the actual planning of your own book.

CHAPTER 2

Designing Your Grimoire

PART OF THE FUN OF CREATING A GRIMOIRE is designing it from the ground up—not just the physical form, but also the interior, the decoration, and the sections for the subjects; all these things call for thought as you plan them out. You'll need to consider your current habits, past successes or failures in creating ways to record your spiritual journey, your intentions in how to use this version, and so much more. Like building a new room, you have to sit down and think about what your book is going to be like.

Consider your current methods of recording information. Do you have printouts of interesting articles or rituals you have written? Do you keep a handwritten journal or a dream diary? Does your current system fit your personality or style? Do you want to expand on it and incorporate what you already do, or change it entirely? If you're crafty, this is the ideal way to express that in terms of your spirituality.

Budget is also an important discussion to have with yourself. Not only do you have to take your current budget into account, but you also have to consider your future financial situation as well. Your dreams of a fully realized grimoire won't happen overnight. Don't sink a ton of money into setting it up, especially if you're trying a new system. Start from the ground up: basics first. You can add to it over the years.

Begin by Brainstorming

When you started practicing witchcraft, you may have used any blank book you could find to start recording your work. Now is the time to think about all the ways you could make your ideal grimoire, from the inside to the outside. Take notes as you go to record ideas and inspiration. Dream big, then pick and choose among your ideas, scaling up or down as you need. To begin, think about and define these two terms for yourself:

- *Beautiful*
- *Useful*

Thinking about these two terms can help you pin down vague feelings and give you a guideline or general direction to explore. Remember, beautiful things can be useful, and useful things can be beautiful; the terms aren't contradictory.

You can also start a mood board or vision board, collecting photos or art of books that inspire you during the brainstorming and design process. Pulling potential design elements together like this can help you get a clearer idea of what you want to include, and what doesn't fit. (Don't toss your rejected ideas! You'll most likely have more than one version or volume of your grimoire during your life, and what doesn't work now may be perfect for the next version.)

I suggest that you read through this book first before making concrete decisions. Take notes as you read, of course, but don't jump into making your grimoire feet first before you consider everything this book has to offer. Information you come across in later chapters may impact your design decisions!

You should also start thinking about what type of information you want to include in your grimoire. Review the sections listed in Chapter 1 (and look ahead to Chapters 3, 4, and 5 for more detailed ideas) and consider what specific information you want to include in your own grimoire. This will influence your layout ideas. You may want to design different layouts for each section of your grimoire. Start imagining those layouts. Collect ideas for inspiration and templates.

You'll want to think about what sort of inclusions you want in your grimoire. Inclusions are the things you glue or fasten in, like ticket stubs, postcards, and pamphlets. If scrapbooking appeals to you, you can make use of the aisles and aisles of materials and decoration ideas in craft stores. Look at travel journals online for ideas; these often have all manner of things glued in, like tickets and postcards, but also quick sketches, receipts, scraps of fabric, photos, handwritten pieces, and more.

It's true that starting a huge project like this can be daunting. You might have thoughts like *Don't mess this up*, *It has to be perfect*, or *I'll be locked into whatever I decide to start with*. But here's the reality: You will spill stuff on your grimoire, pages will get torn, and pages will fall out. Your grimoire is a workbook, not a collectible that should sit on a shelf and only be looked at now and again. And if your initial try doesn't work for you—start again. Keep the elements that did work, but try something different where your choices didn't work the way you expected them to.

There's nothing wrong with making a test run grimoire. In fact, if your plans are grand and include expensive supplies and materials, making a smaller version might be a good idea. That way you can discover if your design is what you really want and if it serves your needs.

Choosing the Size

The size of your grimoire is a critical decision that will have to be made early in the process, because it will affect later decisions such as layouts and what form your actual book will take.

For example, are you planning to keep your grimoire at home or carry it around with you? If you plan to keep it in one place, you could go bigger and have sweeping page layouts. If you want to take your grimoire out and about with you, a smaller size will facilitate that.

Another aspect of size to consider is the thickness of the grimoire. Do you want to keep everything in one volume, or perhaps plan your grimoire as a set of separate books containing separate topics that together make a collected grimoire?

As romantic as one large tome filled with spiritual and magical information is, the idea of creating separate books has a lot of merit. It's easier to grab one smaller book and work with it, whether adding info or reading it. You don't have to worry about running out of room in a section of one main book, either; simply begin a new topic-specific book and keep going. On the other hand, it can be hard to decide where to put certain info. Putting the information in multiple places is a perfectly good solution; after all, no one is going to penalize you for duplicating information in your grimoire. Or you can cross-reference, putting the information in one book but adding a note in the other place as to where you chose to place it. (See Chapter 4 for a discussion on indexing and how to keep track of what information is where.)

A Bound Book

A bound book is an aesthetically beautiful choice for a grimoire. You can divide the book into sections and flip back and forth as needed to record your information. A book also sits well on a shelf. But what happens when one section you've divided off fills up, yet the others still have room? This is one of the things you need to consider when designing your grimoire. Here are some options:

SINGLE BOUND BOOK WITH SECTIONS

A single bound book with sections marked is one way to approach the bound book option. As a section is filled, you can set up a second book the same way and continue to record info between the books until all the sections in the first are filled completely, then continue in the second book alone. Make sure you date each entry, and write the overall dates inside the cover so you can keep the books in order.

- **Pros:** You'll use every page. You just need to flip to one section in each book when searching for something.

- **Cons:** Your books will overlap in use, meaning you will have at least two operational at any given time. This isn't a big deal; it's just something to be aware of.

A SET OF BOUND BOOKS

Another option is a set of bound books, where each one is designated to a certain topic. One can be for magical journaling, one for meditation, one to record spells, one to record rituals, one for herbal information, and so forth.

- **Pros:** You won't be dealing with an unwieldy tome. You can replace a single book as it fills up.

- **Cons:** Sometimes it can be hard to separate topics. Cross-referencing can be a bit more challenging when working across separate volumes.

A Binder

A three-ring binder may not feel as romantic as a bound book, but removable pages can be very useful, and a binder with page protectors can go a long way. You can also slip more than one thing in a page protector; for example, having multiple copies of a ritual you use frequently if you practice with others is helpful. Page protectors are also amazing if you've glued a bunch of items to a page, like scrapbooking elements or pressed/dried flowers or plant matter, as they can contain loose bits, and the page sleeves protect the elements from accidental loss.

- **Pros:** You can move sections around as you need to. You can always add more pages when required. You can upgrade to a larger binder if your initial one gets too full.

- **Cons:** Removable pages mean pages can also be misplaced. Sometimes the mechanisms get stuck or broken, and the binder will need to be replaced.

No matter which option you choose, always create an index at the front or back so you know what information is on what page! See Chapter 4 for a discussion and guide to indexing.

> You'll want to give some thought to what you do with loose papers. You will inevitably end up with loose papers and clippings of some kind. If you're using a binder, these can be slipped into page protectors, but if you're using a bound book, you'll have to handle them some other way. You could glue them into the pages in the appropriate section, or you could include an envelope inside the back cover. Remember, though, if you're using a bound book, every page you add will push against the spine, and the outer edge will be pushed open.

A Modular System

There is a very practical and efficient system called the Midori system, named after the brand that is most commonly associated with this style of notebook. It consists of a cover with elastic cords running from the top to the bottom of the spine. You can slip separate insert notebooks around these elastics, which are then held in the cover.

This is an interesting option, because you can swap inserts around as well as replace them separately as they fill up. While the original Traveler's Notebooks by Midori come in a few select sizes, the concept of the cover/insert system has grown far beyond them. If you search *Midori* or *fauxdori* on a craft site, you'll find all sorts of beautifully designed and constructed covers of different sizes. You can buy notebooks to insert separately, and you can usually choose what format of paper you want on the inside: lined, dot grid, blank, and so forth. These covers usually have an elastic cord that wraps around them to keep the entire collection closed. Sometimes they have pockets inside for loose items.

You can also make your own. There are detailed DIY videos available for both covers and inserts, which allow you to design your own according to your needs. If you make your own inserts, you can design the page layout for what you intend to use it for, like pages for ritual records or herbal information. Printing and binding your own inserts is a fun hands-on activity, and you can charge or bless the materials and the construction as you go.

- **Pros:** This is a very versatile system, with the ability to swap inserts as they fill or as your focus changes.

- **Cons:** You won't always have everything in one place. The smaller size can be harder to write in than larger books or binders.

Don't forget bookmarks. Do you want these to be removable or part of the book? Removable markers can fall out, unless they're clip-on or magnetic. Ribbons glued into the back cover can be quick alternatives that will stay put. You can also use a combination of both. Some things you'll refer to often, which merit a more permanent marker, while other things will be temporary or on a project-by-project basis, which can call for a quick marker that can be removed as soon as you're done.

A Pocket Grimoire

A small portable pocket grimoire is a tiny "best of" version of your main grimoire. Carry it with you for prayer, quick reference, and note-taking on the go. A modular multibook kind of system is terrific to use as a pocket grimoire. You can scribble things down in one notebook insert to be recopied in your grimoire at home, consult quick reference information on common correspondences on another insert, browse inspirational quotations and art from another, and keep a fourth for personal notes or to-do ideas. As one notebook gets used up in your pocket grimoire, you can simply swap it for a new one and either file the filled volume with others or copy the information into your main grimoire.

Pocket grimoires are a way to stay in touch with your practice throughout the day. Small versions can be tossed into your backpack or briefcase so they're at hand when an idea crosses your mind or if you need comfort or inspiration. They can also be seen as a rough draft of the material intended for your main grimoire. Things can be scribbled down, crossed out, and otherwise tossed onto the page with the knowledge that it will all be recopied and tidied up later. Sometimes this step allows you to be a bit freer, removing the obstacle of self-imposed perfection that may hobble your self-expression.

A Digital Grimoire

A digital grimoire is exactly what it sounds like: a grimoire in virtual form. This may surprise some green witches, who hold an idealized concept of a witch alone out in nature or who eschew technology in their practice. That's fine; it's a personal choice. But in today's world, where a green witch can operate perfectly well in the heart of a city, ignoring all the possibilities at your disposal is cutting yourself off from a rich wellspring of potential.

A digital grimoire may be the way to go if you have accessibility issues with handwriting, or if you intend to edit the material regularly. It can be the answer if you have anxiety obstacles about planning out sections in a hardbound book. Also, if you're trying to minimize your use of paper, a fully digital grimoire may be for you. Digital grimoires are easily searched using a search function, helping you easily find where you put something.

There's no rule that says you can't create a grimoire that is a combination of print and digital! You can use digital methods of recording rituals and spells, a bound book for your magical journaling, and a binder for your research, correspondence lists, and samples. A grimoire doesn't have to be a single unit. Use whatever combination works for you! You can also type out your spells and rituals, print out what you want, and then keep the physical pages in a binder. Do what works for you, as long as it facilitates keeping your records and building your reference material for your spiritual journey.

There are several ways to go about making a digital grimoire. In essence, you're creating a database of your records and collected information. While it's not a database in the way a programmer might think of it, it's at its foundation a collection of information that is sorted and held for consultation.

A digital grimoire can be searched with a few taps on a keyboard, which is one of its strengths. Not sure where you placed that spell, or what tag you used for information on Mayan deities? Search a keyword, and entries with that word will pop up. The added bonus is that it will also pull up other entries that mention that word, creating a web of potential cross-referencing of ideas within your own records. When making a digital grimoire you could do any of the following:

- Use a productivity app such as Evernote, OneNote, or a similar program
- Use a journaling app
- Use a private blog

Productivity apps allow you to set up folders and subfolders (they may call them something different, but that's essentially how they operate). This allows you to organize your digital grimoire the same way we've discussed already, with sections for rituals, spells, correspondences, study notes, and so forth. It's fluid and in a state of growth all the time, which is exciting. You can copy and paste information (as long as you include your source!), link to online mood boards, upload photos, and have it at your fingertips if you carry a smartphone. Another idea is to set up a private wiki for your information.

Journaling apps tend to default to chronological entries, but if you tag every entry conscientiously, then you should be able to search #rituals or #correspondences and have all the associated entries pop up. You could consider using a journaling app for your spiritual journal portion of your grimoire if you feel more comfortable with a tablet or smartphone than pen and paper for recording dreams, meditation responses, and exercise or activity notes. Tag these, too, so that when you want to find something, it will be as easy as searching keywords.

A private blog would function much like a journaling app, but usually has categories that you can set up as well as tags, so you can assign each entry a category for easy locating in the future. Blogs often have dedicated apps that you can use to facilitate posting. If you're uncomfortable hosting it on the blog platform's site, you can buy your own URL and subscribe to a web hosting service. This allows you to back it up to your own system, too, and manage it however you like.

Whatever software or app you choose to make your digital grimoire, your software ideally should have a tagging system, a search function, an easy way to import other files, and the capability to move and organize documents within a folder.

Like any system, a digital grimoire also has drawbacks. It requires up-to-date software; converting older file formats to newer can alter the way a file displays, which can be frustrating if you worked hard on a specific layout in an older version of the program. If you stop using a certain piece of software, then exporting to a new file format can be a challenge. Drawbacks also include not being able to flip through the pages for inspiration; if you rely on a search function to find things, it can limit the potential for discovery and incidental insight. Your device could run out of power, or the server could be down. If the power goes out, you can't charge your device or access Wi-Fi. There is also the risk of losing access to your files or having them hacked. If your material is oath-bound, this can be serious. Even if it's not, having strangers go through your private records and thoughts is deeply violating.

Here are some things to keep in mind if you keep a digital grimoire:

- It's important to update older files to keep them accessible to newer versions of the software you're using.

- Remember to update your storage methods as your peripherals or main unit evolve or are replaced. You may have burned your grimoire to a CD backup, for example, but your new computer may not have an optical drive.

- *Back up regularly!* Program your system to back up your grimoire files on the first of every month, for example. External hard drives or flash drives can fail; consider backing up to a cloud-based service in addition to an on-site backup.

CHAPTER 3

Creating Your Grimoire

NOW THAT YOU'VE GIVEN THOUGHT to the broader range of decisions concerning your grimoire, you can move on to more specific details of actually creating the book. What do you want your grimoire to look like? What sort of design and layout would work best for you? How do you want to assemble it, and how do you want to organize it?

The practicalities of how you intend to use it will inform your decisions at this stage of your planning. Remember, though, it all comes down to your preferences: what you find beautiful, what you find useful, and what makes you happy when you use it.

Choosing the Right Paper

If you're planning a physical grimoire, paper is something you'll need to consider. Here are a few things to keep in mind while you're in the designing stage of your grimoire.

If you're planning to use a bound book, look at the paper inside it. The lighter the paper, the more difficult it will be to glue things to it (the paper will wrinkle and buckle easily). Also if the paper is light, it is more likely that your ink may bleed through to the second side of the page, making it impossible for you to write on both sides of the paper. Conversely, the thicker the paper, the fewer pages the book will contain, meaning that you'll have to replace it sooner.

Think also about whether you will be handwriting or using a printer. The average weight of copy or inkjet printer paper may be a bit light if you're planning to use paint, markers, or glue, so check the weight on the package. The higher the weight of the paper, the thicker the sheet. Average printer paper is around twenty pounds, while seventy pounds is like light card stock (think the heavy paper that tickets are printed on, or even a light postcard weight). Always check to see the maximum weight of paper your printer can handle too. The brightness of the white of the paper may also be an issue. Brightness describes how much light reflects off the paper. Average printer paper has a brightness of about 80. The higher the number, the brighter the white will appear, because it reflects more light.

In the design process, you may choose a variety of papers. If you plan to glue things to paper or paint in your grimoire, a heavier weight may be a good choice for those pages, while regular inkjet printer paper may serve for the others.

You can also look into making your own paper. It's actually easier than it sounds. Use the following activity to make an herbal paper for writing your spells.

MAKING HERBAL PAPER

Making your own paper is a great way to involve the energy of herbs and flowers in your spellcraft, as well as to be able to empower your spellcraft from beginning to end to really set your intentions. Please note that this project calls for a blender. Pick one up at a thrift store; don't use a good one for this. A thrift store food processor could work as well. If you want tinted paper, add a few drops of food coloring to the blender. Start with one or two and blend; less is more!

> **NOTE** Writing on this paper could be tricky. A felt-tip pen might bleed, and a very fine ballpoint pen could scratch the paper surface instead of laying down ink. Experiment with scraps of the paper to see how different inks react before using a pairing in an actual spell or other magical situation.

WHAT YOU NEED
- Herbal inclusions keyed to your goal (see Chapter 5)
- 8" × 10" wooden picture frame with glass insert
- Screening (mosquito screen made of nylon or wire)
- Heavy stapler
- Mortar and pestle
- Shredded paper (approximately 2 handfuls to make 1 sheet of paper)
- Bucket or deep waterproof container

- Water
- Blender
- 2 or 3 towels (old bath towels work well for this)
- Blotting paper (newspaper, craft paper, etc.)
- Heavy book
- Envelope for storage

WHAT TO DO

1. Choose herbs and/or flowers to incorporate in your paper according to your magical goal.

2. Prepare the screen mold for your paper: Remove the glass insert of the picture frame and set it aside to use later in this activity. Take your screening and stretch it across the back of the 8" × 10" picture frame. Staple it securely in place.

3. Grind the dried plant matter well with a mortar and pestle or crumble the dried flowers.

4. Take the shredded paper and soak it in a bucket of water for 15–20 minutes. (If your shredded paper is thicker or heavier, it can take longer.)

5. Fill the blender halfway full with water, then add a spoonful of the soaked paper; close the blender and process it. Stop, add another spoonful of soaked paper, and repeat. Don't overload the blender with just paper slurry; it can burn the motor out. Add the dried herbs to the blender and stir or pulse quickly.

6. Spoon the pulp out on the screen as evenly as possible. Put the glass insert you set aside earlier on top and press down gently. Set the frame on a folded towel to catch drips of water as it drains.

7. After the immediate water has drained, lift off the glass and carefully flip the mold over onto folded towels. Lift the mold off, then cover the wet paper sheet with another towel and press.

8. An easy way to dry the paper evenly and without buckling is to make a lasagna-type stack. Start with blotting paper, lay the handmade paper on top, cover with more blotting paper, and so forth. Put a heavy book on top to press the stack down. Check the pressed paper every day and remove it when it's dry. How long that will be depends on how wet your slurry was, what your weather is like, and how absorbent your blotting paper is. If you find that the blotting paper is damp and your handmade paper isn't dry yet, remove the damp blotting sheets and replace them with a fresh set.

9. Store in an envelope marked with the date and the ingredients, along with the intention set during the papermaking process.

If you have paper slurry left over, drain it in a sieve, squeeze out excess water, and let it dry. You can use it again the next time you make paper.

You might want to look into ecologically friendly papers. Paper manufacture uses a lot of wood pulp, and a lot of energy goes into cutting trees, transporting them, and processing them. Reusing paper cuts down on environmental impact and has a smaller carbon footprint. You can also look into paper made from wood alternative, like wheat straw or sugarcane. Be aware, though, that the longevity and archival quality of these papers hasn't been tested to the same degree wood-based paper has.

As your grimoire is also a form of art and self-expression, you could dye the paper you use for specific pages. Dipping a sheet of paper into a shallow pan of cooled strong tea or coffee can tint it to a parchment color. If you're interested in other colors, look into making natural dyes. For example, boiling 1 cup of mashed berries with 1 tablespoon of salt in 2 cups of water will create a reddish dye stock; and 2 cups of chopped grass and leaf clippings with 1 tablespoon of salt in 2 cups of water will create a variety of hues from green through gold, depending on the types used. Bring these mixtures to a boil, then reduce heat and simmer for about 45–60 minutes. Cool the mixture, then strain it. Pour the dye stock into a shallow pan (a baking tray or 9" × 13" pan is ideal) and lower the sheet into it, gently pressing down if it floats stubbornly. Lift it out and lay it on a cooling rack over newspaper, or pin it up on a clothesline to dry.

You can play with all sorts of other natural materials to add color to your paper:

- Chopped red cabbage yields a purple/red tone; add 1 table-spoon of baking soda to shift it to a blue.
- Beets make a really deep ruby-garnet red dye stock, but when dry the paper will be pale rose.

- Yellow onion skins yield an ochre.
- Ground turmeric yields a rich golden yellow.
- Washed whole avocado pits yield a gentle pink.

Experiment with scraps of paper, writing down the dye stock used on the sample once it is dry. You can also freeze prepared dye stock and use it at a later time.

Finding the Perfect Ink and Pens

If you're printing your grimoire out from a computer or photocopying certain things, you won't have much of a choice concerning the ink you use. On the other hand, if you are handwriting it, you can tailor your ink to your goals.

If you intend to use a commercial pen, look for one that has waterproof ink. Your grimoire could be used in several situations where water or oils are also used, so waterproof ink is a good investment against potential spills.

Good fountain pens can be found for under $30. You can use pre-filled cartridges with them, but I vastly prefer using a refillable converter instead. It allows me to choose what color ink to use for specific things. Fountain pens are flexible and versatile, and they're a good investment if you plan to do written spells frequently. The nibs come in a range of widths, from extra-fine through italic stubs; take a look at the pen strokes online at fountain pen retailers to choose one that appeals to you.

If you do decide to use a fountain or dip pen, you may have to buy a better quality paper for it. Regular cheap copy or printer paper often is too thin, making the ink feather, or creep into the fibers around the initial pen stroke. Sugarcane-based paper is friendly to fountain pen ink (and eco-friendly), and you can find high-quality paper created specifically for fountain pens by stationery shops. If you're writing in a notebook, test the pen and ink on a page in the back before committing to writing a long piece in it. Thicker nibs will lay down more ink in a stroke, and the risk of the ink feathering increases.

If fountain pens feel too complicated, try a dip pen. Dip pens can be found at fountain pen retailers as well as many art stores in calligraphy sections. However, be careful what ink you use. Dip pens intended for drawing often use Chinese ink, which will clog a fountain pen, and bottles of drawing inks are also not optimal for fountain pens. (To complicate matters, you can draw with fountain pen ink, using brushes or pens.)

Inks for fountain dip pens come in a dizzying rainbow of colors, shades, hues, and finishes. Shimmer inks with sparkle in them can make the experience of writing a grimoire entry feel more magical. Some inks are expensive, while others are very affordable. Some online retailers sell samples of inks, enough to fill a pen once or twice depending on the size of the converter. At only a dollar or two each, you can amass a selection of colors and brands to test and use as you like. If you find you click with a certain color and manufacturer and plan to use it frequently, you can invest in a larger bottle of it.

MAKING A QUILL PEN

Quill pens are a fun project that can make a spell or written prayer extra special. Like with other toolmaking, making your own quill pen is an exercise in concentration and focus. The pen can also be used as a representation of the element of air, which is associated with intellect and communication, which in turn are both aspects of writing. A quill pen, made from a feather, carries deep air energy.

For this activity you'll need a large feather, usually a primary flight feather. The shaft needs to be sturdy and large enough to cut into a nib shape. Traditionally, quills were cut from goose feathers, but turkey feathers or feathers from another large bird would be fine. Crow feathers were used for very fine work. In the interest of being as ethically responsible as possible, look for naturally shed or lost feathers instead of buying them at a craft shop. If there is a farm nearby, contact the establishment to ask if you can collect shed feathers.

Quill pens used to be stripped of all the barbs, leaving just the shaft, although for a time there was a fashion for leaving the barbs at the tip. Stripping the barbs allows for the writer to see what they're writing more easily. Before quills, reeds used to be cut into pens, but feather shafts were gentler on parchment.

WHAT YOU NEED
- Feather
- Dish soap (antibacterial is ideal)
- Water
- Sharp craft knife (such as an X-Acto knife)

- Cutting board
- Scissors
- Fine-tip marker

WHAT TO DO

1. Scrub the feather with dish soap and water. Feathers can carry germs, so washing it thoroughly cleans it not only of dirt and oils but also of bacteria.

2. Rinse well. Soak the feather overnight in clean water to help soften the shaft, making it easier to cut.

3. Dry the feather. Using the craft knife and the cutting board, cut off the bottom of the feather shaft to make a flat end (this will be the tip). Do this carefully to avoid splitting the shaft; a split will render the feather useless as a pen. (If you do split the shaft, don't throw away the pen; you can use it as a nib holder instead. See the note at the end of this activity.)

4. With the scissors, trim away the barbs closest to the base and up about 3"–4", leaving the shaft bare. This is the part of the quill that will rest in your hand.

5. Take the quill in your hand and hold it as if you were writing with it. Turn the quill until it's resting comfortably in your hand. Take note of the side that is closest to you; this will be the back. With the fine-tip marker, draw a diagonal, slightly curved line on one side of the shaft, starting a millimeter or two away from the front and curving up toward the back, about a centimeter up from the base.

6. Place the feather on its side with the line facing up on the cutting board. Carefully trim the excess part of the shaft away within the curved line. You may have to roll the feather 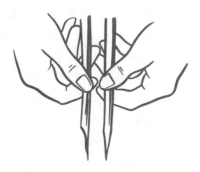 slightly to cut the other side. Start by trimming a bit, then a bit more, rather than trying to bear down and cut it all at once. Go slowly, and watch your fingers. Feather shafts can be hard to cut, even after soaking the feather overnight.

7. When you have trimmed the excess away, lay the feather on its front so the back of the nib area faces up. Carefully cut a slit a couple of millimeters long in the middle of the nib. This allows the nib to flex and lay down the ink easier.

8. Test the quill by dipping the nib into ink and drawing lines on a piece of paper with it. Make lines and curves to get used to how the nib performs. When you're finished with the quill, dip the nib in water and wipe it dry.

> **NOTE** If the shaft splits at any point during the trimming process, buy a metal dip pen nib from an art supply shop and slip it into the split shaft. Wrap the area where the nib and shaft meet tightly with thread, add drops of a waterproof adhesive like strong glue to secure it, then allow it to dry completely. The quill thus becomes a nib holder.

INK AND PAPER COLORS

The color of your ink and paper can be significant too. You may choose to record information about herbs and plant lore in green or brown, for example. Ritual work or worship may be recorded in blue. Dream records may be purple. It's up to you and your color preferences and your personal color associations. If you're writing magic, choosing the color to support your intention is an extra layer of energy you can draw on to reinforce your intent.

Choosing color because it's pretty is absolutely fine too. Your grimoire should reflect your love and joy in the energy of the world and the spirituality of your practice. Happiness is important, and you should enjoy using your grimoire.

FONTS

You may think that fonts are exclusively a digital issue, but they are not. Choosing how to write down your information is important in handwritten grimoires as well. What font you choose to write in may depend on your mood. You may print things clearly one day and do quick cursive the next. You might do some pages in elaborate flowing script and scratch out quick notes on the next.

No matter how you write, it's always a good idea to consider it beforehand. How will you be using the information you're about to write in your grimoire? Do you plan to read from it for recipes, rituals, or spells? Is the information you're entering going to be consulted quickly, therefore needing to be clear on immediate access? Questions like this will help you decide how to write out specific information.

Adding Decorations and Illustrations

Part of the fun of creating your own grimoire is being able to design it from the very start. That includes choosing illustrations. There are no rules about how to decorate or illustrate your grimoire, so enjoy this part. You can cut photos out of magazines or calendars, print out beautiful things that inspire you from the Internet, or draw your own images. You can play with color, illustrating with abstract shapes and designs. Perhaps you can take a photo of your seasonal celebration ritual setup, print it, and glue it in to have a visual record of how you celebrated in addition to recording notes. Art can elevate your grimoire to an inspirational piece of its own accord. Going through your grimoire should be an enjoyable experience!

Including photos or illustrations of herbs, flowers, and trees in your reference section can be an excellent memory aid. You can also press samples of the actual plant matter and then glue them in or slip them into a glassine envelope that you glue in instead. This way, if the dried plant matter crumbles, it's contained.

Gluing things into your grimoire will make the pages thicker than they already are. If you're using a bound book of some kind, that means that eventually it won't close properly. This may not bother some people, but others may find it problematic. One solution is to remove a blank page for every page to which you glue something. This allows space for the now-thicker page. If you use a binder, this won't be an issue for you.

Original art is beautiful in a grimoire. Don't worry that you're not good enough. Don't hold back because you don't consider yourself an artist. What comes from your heart is beautiful. Realistic illustration is only one small corner of the world of art. Experiment with colors, indulge in your fascination with pretty washi tape, and experiment with papercutting. Look at art journals on *Instagram* or *Flickr*; you'll see that the small artworks in daily journals are often sketchy or created with dabs and quick movements.

Judging a Book by Its Cover

It isn't shallow to feel that aesthetics are important. How you feel when you see or handle a tool influences how you interact with it. The more positive you feel when you approach the grimoire, the more likely you are to work with it. And that's important, because your grimoire is one of the most important tools you'll ever work with. You want to be as happy with your grimoire as possible in order to minimize your resistance to recording your work. (There will be resistance; we're only human, and record-keeping often feels like a chore. See Chapters 7 and 8 for an exploration of record-keeping and journaling.)

Aesthetics extend to the interior of your grimoire too. If the layout you've chosen no longer works for you, develop a new one based on your observations of how the previous one worked and fell short for you. Evolution in your grimoire's presentation is perfectly natural; you grow and develop, after all, and your grimoire is a reflection of you and your journey.

You are not limited to the default look of the book or binder you chose as your grimoire. If you are happy with its aesthetic presentation, then that's terrific. If you've chosen it for practicality, then enjoy personalizing the cover. The easiest way to customize a book or binder is to make a cover for it. If you had to cover your textbooks in school, then you're already familiar with this process. (If not, use a search engine to look for phrases like *how to make a cover for a book* and specify either paper or fabric to get an idea of how to go about it.) Crafting a removable cover is ideal because you can swap out the blank book inside it once it's full. A removable cover is also a good idea in case your binder fails (the rings can become bent, stop snapping shut properly, or jam). Make sure you can trade out your grimoire binder if that happens.

Fabric covers can be personalized with ribbon, lace, glue-on gems, iron-on patches, or fabric paint. Paper covers can be decorated with paint, scrapbooking materials, collages, pressed flowers, or anything you like. Don't forget to cover the paper cover with clear contact paper to protect it once you've finished it.

Privacy Concerns

Do you live in an environment where you feel that your grimoire may be unsafe? Designing and decorating the exterior might need to take this into account. You may have to camouflage it to avoid it attracting attention. Make the inside as witchy as you like if you're forced to keep the outside unobtrusive.

If you're concerned about people getting into it, consider a lock. Some books come with locks, but they're usually very weak, and often very slender. Check your local hardware store for hasps and small padlocks, and use a strong adhesive like Gorilla Glue to attach the hasps to your grimoire's front and back cover. Carry one key with you and hide another key.

Digital grimoires should be password-locked, no matter what form they take. The passcode for your phone or tablet might be enough, but if you can add an extra passcode for the app or website, so much the better.

Book Blessing

Like with any other tool, you will want to cleanse and bless your new grimoire. Cleanse it according to your favorite method that doesn't include water. If water is your favorite element with which to purify or cleanse things, experiment with an ultrasonic cool mist essential oil diffuser; you can add a drop or two of your favorite essential oil you use for cleansing, or use it with plain water. (For various cleansing or purifying techniques, see three of my other books: *The Green Witch, Protection Spells*, or *Spellcrafting*.) If the idea of cleansing the grimoire after putting so much love and energy into making it bothers you, cleanse the book and basic materials before you begin, then bless the finished product.

Here are two aspects of a blessing: a written blessing to insert into the book and a small ritual to dedicate your grimoire to your use. You can use one or both.

WRITING A BLESSING

Writing a book blessing is an enjoyable task. Sit down in a quiet spot and light your favorite incense, or diffuse a drop of your favorite oil. Light a candle or a few. Prepare your favorite beverage and a plate of snacks. Set your phone to Do Not Disturb mode. The idea is to be as comfortable and content as possible.

There are two ways to do this. The first is to work on scrap paper, writing and rewriting your blessing until you're happy with it, then copying it into your grimoire. The second is to take a little while to meditate, then write a stream-of-consciousness blessing directly in the book, as inspiration directs you.

In case you're worried, a blessing doesn't have to be poetry, either rhyming or blank verse; it can be prose if that is what you're more comfortable with. Here's a sample blessing:

> *Grimoire,*
> *Be for me the container of my secrets,*
> *The aggregate of my knowledge,*
> *The well of my inspiration.*
> *May my work be blessed by you,*
> *My records safely held,*
> *And defended.*

May you contain my energy safely,
Storing it against my future need,
And may the knowledge you hold
Support me as I follow my path
And honor Nature.

You can also write a companion piece for grimoire protection if you feel your grimoire should have one.

If you want, you can make a small blessing charm with two small pieces of fabric and an assortment of protection herbs between them, then attach it to the inside of the cover. Or sew a bookmark out of two long, narrow rectangles of fabric, with the herbs inside.

SEWING A BLESSING CHARM

This is an easy activity that is entirely personalized. Choose a color of fabric that you associate with blessing and/or protection, or that complements your grimoire's color. You can use patterned fabric or plain. Choose whatever herbs or flowers you like to put inside it. For an easy version, use hot glue to seal the bookmark closed instead of sewing it.

To figure out how much fabric you need, measure your grimoire from the top of the cover to the bottom. Use this measurement for the length of the bookmark. Make the strip 5 inches wide. This will yield a bookmark that is approximately 2 inches wide.

WHAT YOU NEED

- Dried herbs and flowers you associate with blessing (e.g., lavender, sandalwood, cedar, rose, etc.); total approximately 1 tablespoon
- Small bowl
- Rectangle of fabric (see previous note for how to measure)
- Sewing pins
- Needle and thread (color your choice)
- Iron and ironing board (optional)

WHAT TO DO

1. Choose your herbs and flowers. Use a pinch of each to begin with, adding them to the bowl, then see how much you have. Add pinches until your total is approximately 1 tablespoon of your blend.

2. Charge your herbal blend, empowering it with blessing and/or protection.

3. Fold your strip of fabric in half lengthwise, right sides together. Pin along the edges.

4. Sew one short edge and the long edge closed with a running stitch. Make sure the stitches are small and close together so the dried herbs won't slip out.

5. Turn the bookmark right-side out. Press it flat if you have an iron.

6. Slip the dried herbs into the bookmark.

7. Fold the raw edges of the open end inside the bookmark. Sew it shut.

8. Place it between the pages of your grimoire.

> **NOTE** If your fabric is very lightweight, you may be concerned about the herbs slipping to the bottom. To prevent this, you can shake and smooth the bookmark until the herbs seem distributed evenly, then sew a seam along the middle. Sew two or three seams across the bookmark, creating self-contained channels that each hold some of the herbs in place.

DEDICATION RITUAL

Here is a sample dedication ritual for your grimoire. First, set up your workspace according to your preferred manner and have your grimoire ready. When you have begun your ritual as per your customary practice, center and ground, then take your grimoire in your hands and say:

> *Spirits of Nature,*
> *Bless this book that I have prepared to be my companion as I travel the path of the green witch.*
> *May I be inspired as I write in it.*
> *May the information herein serve to support me in my spiritual development.*
> *May truths reveal themselves to me as I review my writings.*
> *May this grimoire support me in my work to become the best person I can be,*
> *And in being the steward of Nature.*
> *May this grimoire and my practice with it serve Nature in the best of ways.*
> *May both this book and I be blessed.*

Starting Your Grimoire Off Right

Another way to dedicate your book is by including a list of things that are important to you and writing it into the first few pages. Think of it as coding the book, keying it to specific goals or values you hold. If you work with deities, include a list of them, with key words associated with their areas of correspondence or a phrase declaring your allegiance to each and what they stand for.

Whether you do or don't work with deities, an important element to include at this stage is a list of the values you uphold. Do you honor respect, justice, and honesty? This is where to declare your support of these things. In a way, you're writing affirmations for your journey with this grimoire.

With all these details (and the ones to follow in Chapter 4), you may wonder if your grimoire will ever be finished. It will not. A grimoire is a living, evolving, mutable tool and resource. Keep in mind that it reflects you at different stages of your journey. Documenting that journey as well as collecting as much information as you feel you need to broaden and deepen your understanding of the energy of the natural world is what working with your grimoire is about. Consider your grimoire your partner and a work in progress—just as you are.

CHAPTER 4

Setting Up Your Grimoire

ONCE YOU'VE MADE THE DECISIONS regarding the design of your grimoire, you'll have to think about what information to start including in it. This can entail copying in what information you've already collected to date as well as planning new sections to begin. In a way, you already thought about what information to include in your grimoire on a basic level when you were deciding how to format your grimoire (binder, one book with divisions, one book with information written in it as it comes, a set of separate books devoted to different topics, and so on). This chapter will help you decide not only what to include in your grimoire but how to organize those things in the most practical and functional ways.

What to Include in Your Grimoire

To help you begin, a good exercise is to think about what information you draw on frequently. Here's a short list of questions to ask yourself:

- What information do I want to consult regularly?
- What information do I want to record regularly?
- What material do I want to be included in my grimoire?

Let's look at each of these concerns individually.

INFORMATION YOU WANT TO CONSULT

You probably have a library of books on witchcraft and spiritual paths. Some may be reference books that you pull off the shelf regularly. Is there information in them that you could transfer to your grimoire to eliminate consulting multiple sources? Would putting the information in your grimoire be more efficient? This part also covers information you collect about plants, trees, flowers, herbs, stones, and the correspondences of other natural things that you might draw on.

INFORMATION YOU WANT TO RECORD

Information you want to record could cover a dream diary, meditation journal, gratitude journal, spells, recipes, and rituals. It can cover experiments as well, like testing the energy of a new blend of herbs or oils.

MATERIAL YOU WANT TO INCLUDE

This isn't the same as information you regularly consult. This question asks about what other information you'd like to be part of your grimoire so that it reflects you more accurately. You could include your sources of inspiration (people, music, concepts) and create a body of inspirational material. This includes such things as affirmations, photos, pretty pressed flowers or leaves, art, inspiring extracts from books, and anything else that evokes the feeling that you associate with green witchcraft. It's also nice to record prayers or poetry that are particularly meaningful to you.

Design Space for Recording Your Practice

One of the most important sections of your grimoire is going to be where you record your experiences. There are two parts to this record-keeping section.

The first is your record of spells, rituals, and divination. Recording these is critical. Not only does it keep track of what you've done and when, but it allows you a way to review and analyze your work to see what effects it has and a way to evaluate success and failure, and it also provides you with a way to track your progress. This is one of the most critical things you can do as a green witch. It may not sound fun or witchy, but it's immensely valuable if you're going to understand your own processes, weak areas, and spiritual development.

For more on why and how to record these, plus templates for record sheets, see Chapter 7.

The second part is your personal magical journal. This is where you record your ideas, thoughts, dreams, and meditations. It's where you can reflect, work out your emotions, and argue out your passions and your anger. All these are part of you, and they deserve a place in your journal.

Self-reflection isn't an easy task, but it's important for personal growth. If you don't engage in self-reflection, you're cutting off a valuable source of deeper understanding of your own interaction with the energies around you and the world at large. The more you know, the more precisely you can work on improving and enriching that relationship.

Organizing Your Content

Once you know the sections you want in your grimoire, it's time to think about what order you want them in. Do you want information first, and your record and journal sections in the second half? The other way around? Information, records, then journaling? Do you want information and records in one book and journal entries in a separate one? Do you want to eschew sections entirely and use each page as it comes, to reflect a chronological evolution of your spirituality?

There is no right or wrong answer. If you've chosen a binder, then you can move sections around as you want to, using page dividers to clearly mark where a new section begins. If you're using a bound book, your options are a little more limited. You're not married to the system you start with, however. There isn't a rule that says you can't update your system if you discover your initial plan doesn't work as well in practice as it did in theory. You don't even have to wait till your first book is filled up.

Whatever way you choose to order your content, there is one important thing to do: Keep track of where all that information is. And to do that effectively, you need to construct an index.

Finding Things: The Importance of an Index

There is nothing more frustrating than knowing you noted down information but not knowing where you put it. As you assemble information in your grimoire, you'll inevitably come up against the problem of locating exactly where you wrote down a snippet of insight. Fortunately, there are ways to construct an index for your grimoire that are flexible enough to reflect whatever method(s) of construction you've decided on.

The easiest way to set up an index is to set aside a few blank pages at the front or back of your book. Number the pages of your grimoire. As you fill them, write the contents of the pages down on your index page(s). For example, entries in the index might read like this:

PAGE 17: *ethics of wildcrafting and foraging in public spaces*
PAGE 18: *record of spell for abundant harvest 29 July 2019*

PAGE 20: *recipe for calming bath infusion*
PAGES 21–25: *Record of maple tree meditation 07 December 2019*

To use this system with a binder, insert blank pages at the beginning of each section. Number the existing pages per section. For example, on the pages in the Records section, write *1*, *2*, and so on; on the corresponding Records index page, list the pages as *Records-1*, *Records-2*, and so forth. As you add pages to a section, add the page numbers to the section's index.

> If you have everything in one book, consider color-coding the section topics and using different colors of pen or pencil to write the page's information in the index. This will help you find certain topics in the index quickly.

If you use separate books for each topic, put an index in each. I also suggest making a master index in a separate notebook all its own. Over time your collection of books will grow unwieldy. It will be easier to flip through the pages of one book to ascertain the location of the information you're looking for than to sit down with an entire pile of books. It is strongly suggested that you use color-coding for a master index book like this, and as you start new books, clearly identify each with a label giving the subject, which volume of that subject the book is, and the date it was started. When the book is full, add the date it ended as well. Here's an example:

HERBAL CORRESPONDENCES 2
March 2018–January 2020

The other reason creating an independent index is a good idea is because sometimes you won't remember which book you recorded something in. Over time your subjects can blur. If you dreamed a strong suggestion to use lavender for financial assistance, for example, do you choose to put it in your dream journal or in your herbal correspondence book?

There's no rule against recording the same information in more than one place. It can get confusing, though, if you do it too often. Consider the master index idea instead.

Common Reference Information in Grimoires

Now that you have brainstormed your ideas and concepts, know what order you want to arrange your sections in, and have started an index, it's time to take a look at some common information that is generally included in grimoires.

There is a lot of reference information in this section for you to either copy or use as an example of how to include information when setting up your own. Consider this section as part of your own grimoire: an extension of it, or a foundation for you to build on.

RECIPES

It's good to have a basic recipe for things you'll make up on a regular basis, like salves, bath salts, infused oils, sprinkling powders, and herbal incense—not the full recipe, such as for a specific goal, but a basic foundation that you can then add your chosen magical ingredients to in order to code it to your objective. Even just noting down proportions can save you time.

MOON ENERGY INFORMATION

Lunar energy is one of the key energies used in witchcraft, and green witchcraft is no different. Using moon phases is one of the most common methods by which magical work is planned and performed. The general rule is that attraction, or growth magic, is performed in the first half of the lunar month, when the moon appears to be increasing in the sky. Banishing, or magic associated with decrease or reduction, is performed in the second half of the cycle, when the moon appears to shrink away in the sky. That's a broad generalization, but good enough for off-the-cuff work.

The cycle can be divided into more precise sections, however. This is the kind of information that is good to record in your grimoire. This basic information is good to start with, and then you can carry on your own investigations for your personal interpretations.

- **New moon:** The very first sliver of moon seen in the sky is called the new moon. This is technically a couple of days into the cycle, but in relation to our perception of the moon, it qualifies as the beginning. The new moon is appropriately associated with beginnings, the seeds of something that will come to fruition later. It is a good time for setting intentions. It is also a good time to plant.

- **Waxing moon:** *Waxing* means "growing," and that is exactly what the moon seems to be doing in the first half of its cycle. As its light increases in the sky, the lunar energy shifts more to attraction, expansion, and growth. This is a time to do work on ongoing projects that need support in their development. Prosperity, creativity, and learning are all areas to work on during the waxing moon. The waxing gibbous moon is close to full. If you've been working on an incremental spell or project and are aiming to have the final step happen when the full moon arrives, to bring the spell to completion, then the gibbous moon is your penultimate step. It's the heavy, gravid, pregnant energy that is almost entirely ripe. It's very rich energy.

- **Full moon:** This is the energy everyone reaches for, assuming it's the best for whatever they're doing. And in general, the full moon is a great catch-all time to power your magical work. It is about fruition, success, and culmination. It is powerful healing energy (more on that in a moment). It is an excellent time to harvest plants. The full moon is excellent for blessings, confirmations and rituals for rites of passage such as parenthood, and so forth. If you are working healing magic, the full moon can function in different ways. You can use it to power growth and rapid healing. If you are looking to decrease symptoms or the presence of disease or illness, the full moon is a good time to begin your magical work; then continue through the waning half of the moon's cycle, which is associated with decreasing.

- **Waning moon:** *Waning* means "decreasing or fading away," and that's what our perception of the moon tells us is happening as the shadow of the earth passes across it. As the moon's light decreases, the energy it holds turns to energy sympathetic to decreasing, reducing, or banishing things. Areas of correspondence particularly sensitive to this energy include healing where the focus is on removing something, minimizing opposition, and removing obstacles. It is also good for reducing stress and evening out overactivity. The lunar energy of the third quarter is winding down. Like the waxing gibbous moon, the waning gibbous is close to full, but on the waning side of it. It's a very rich time.

- **Dark moon:** *Dark moon* is the term for the part of the lunar phase where you cannot see the moon in the sky at all, because the sunlight doesn't reach the side we see. The dark moon energy is good for introspection, preparation for future work, and nourishing your spirit. Quiet, restorative self-care is a good thing to work on at this time. Think of the dark moon as a winter period, where the earth rests and rejuvenates before moving into action again.

Take a need and start working to attract what you're lacking in the waxing gibbous period into the full moon. Then flip the intention and work to reduce the need in the waning gibbous period. This takes advantage of the richest lunar energy available to you.

SOLAR ENERGY INFORMATION

The sun is bright, energizing, and warm. It fosters life and growth. It is life-giving, and without it we'd be dead. The sun is associated with health, action, and success. It's considered a much more active energy than the moon, which doesn't mean better or more powerful; it's just different. Humanity is solar powered, in a way; we need sunlight in order to produce vitamin D, which is responsible for helping our immune system's function and helping regulate mood. The winter blues are a real thing, and may be related to decreased sunlight in the Northern Hemisphere.

The Daily Solar Cycle

The sun's daily cycle is much quicker than the moon's cycle, so if you're looking to do focused work following an increase-peak-decrease pattern, using the sun and its energy can be very effective.

- **Sunrise** is a time of beginnings. It is an excellent time for setting intentions, working on affirmations, and launching new projects.

- **Morning** is a time of increasing strength, good for working on creative issues and other areas that require expansion in some way.

- **Noon** is considered midday, but your clock doesn't always accurately reflect the actual point of the cycle. Instead, check the time of sunrise and of sunset, and figure out how many hours of daylight there are. Divide that by two, and you'll have a better idea of when the sun will be at its peak.

(This is particularly important if you live in a place where daylight saving time is employed. Moving a clock's setting doesn't change what's happening in the sky.)

- **Afternoon** sees the sun gradually lowering in the sky. It is a time to work on reducing or minimizing things.

- **Sunset** is a good time to address bringing things to completion, putting things away, and closing something's presence or impact.

There are secondary phases in the daily solar cycle. False dawn, for example, is the light that grows in the night sky without the sun actually being in sight. Twilight occurs after the sun has set, but the sun's light still illuminates your world. These are liminal times, when it is not entirely day or night. They are magical and can be very spiritual and transformative. Think about them and come up with your own associations.

The Seasonal Solar Cycle

The sun also travels on a grander scale, giving us the seasons. The winter sun possesses a different energy than the summer sun, for example; it appears to be in a different place in the sky, at a different angle. The earth's axial tilt means that as we orbit, the surface of the earth moves closer and farther away from the sun, which results in a temperature shift that varies through the seasonal cycle. Like with the moon cycle, there is a waxing and waning pattern.

- **Winter** energies are quiet, slow energies. It is a time of hibernation, of recouping energy after exhaustion.

- **Spring** energies are creative, full of potential; they are about planting seeds for future harvesting.

- **Summer** energies are expansive, fertile, and healthy.

- **Fall** energies are about harvest, abundance, and preparing to bring the cycle to a close, winding down in preparation for rest.

ELEMENTS AND QUARTERS

Information on the four elements and their associated quarters and cardinal directions is also commonly found in grimoires. Green witchcraft rests very firmly on direct experience with the elements as they manifest in nature.

The elements are often considered very specific energies, and purer than other materials because they are the building blocks of the rest of nature. For this reason, the elements are often used to power magic on their own; the spirit of the element itself is drawn on.

Earth

Earth is perhaps the element most often associated with green witchcraft. Green is the color we associate with the natural world, with its grass and plants and trees. Earth energy is associated with stability, abundance, healing, balance, strength, and production. The earth provides us with food and shelter, and we are creatures of the earth. We rely on one another; with care and attention, the relationship between humanity and earth is mutually beneficial. In magic, plants, trees, and stones all carry earth energy at their heart.

Air

Air energy surrounds us. Wind carries pollen and seeds, enabling nature to spread. It also carries birdsong and the sounds of nature to our ears, and the scents of the world around us. In magic, we use air in the form of feathers, fans, sacred breath, essential oils, scented flowers, and incense in various forms. Interestingly, most of these require a partnership or relationship with another element. Air is difficult to observe on its own; we see or feel its effects in the context of a reagent. We feel wind on our skin; we see incense smoke rising in idle spirals above the censer; we see waves and whitecaps on the surface of the sea. We can smell the lovely scent given from a flower. The feather of a bird reminds us that a bird uses its body in partnership with air to travel. It is perhaps key to remember that the absence of air is what would cause us to best understand its presence previous to that absence. In other words, you don't appreciate or notice it until it's gone.

Fire

Fire is associated with action, passion, energy, and destruction—not destruction in a negative sense, but in the sense that sometimes you have to utterly deconstruct something before you can rebuild. One technique to control advancing wildfire is to set up a controlled burn in its path. The goal is to remove fuel to starve and stop the fire from traveling any farther via controlled destruction.

Fires are an essential part of an ecosystem's life cycle; they play an ecological role key to regeneration and growth. In a forest, fire releases nutrients in the leaf litter on the forest floor, and it also thins the forest canopy to allow sunlight to reach places previously in shade, stimulating growth. Grassland and scrub fires have similar benefits. Fires can be caused by lightning, but some are deliberately set and controlled by rangers or forest management agencies. If natural, forest services aim to optimize the benefits while minimizing damage. There's an entire science to it.

Uncontrolled fire is a different matter. The power and destructive ability of fire can quickly grow out of control. On one hand, we use fire (or a modern derivative of it) to keep us warm and cook our food. On the other, it can consume both if we are careless, leaving us cold, without shelter, and hungry. This is why we work to remain in control of fire, bearing responsibility for how we manage it.

Water

Water is associated with healing, transformation, purification, cleansing, consecration, and being in connection with your deep psyche. As with air, we cannot live without water. Water is often thought of as a calm energy, but spring flooding tells a different story, as do hurricanes and tsunamis. (Many natural disasters are caused by more than one element; a tsunami is generally triggered by underwater earthquakes, while hurricanes are air and water.) Water sources were often considered holy places; springs and wells were locations where you could speak to deity or nature spirits. Large bodies of water aren't the only water sources; rainfall and snowfall also yield water for magical use.

An easy, straightforward way to bless water for use in spiritual practice is to hold your hands over a cup or bowl of water. Center yourself, ground (connect your center to the earth's energy), then draw up energy into your core. Allow it to flow down your arms and out your hands to energize the water. You can add a "flavor" to this energy if you like, coding it for a specific purpose such as healing or purifying by focusing on that goal while you channel it into the water. Another quick way to make blessed water is to add a pinch of salt to it, give it a quick stir with intention, and concentrate on imbuing it with your energy.

TECHNIQUES FOR CREATING SACRED SPACE

Creating sacred space is the act of formally recognizing or designating an area as blessed and/or protected, intended for magical or spiritual use. Another term for it would be *sanctification*. All nature is sacred and blessed, of course, but the act of formally declaring a specific area as sacred for the purpose of spellcraft or an act of honoring is an act of respect. It also reaffirms in your own mind that your action is sacred, reinforcing your connection to the spiritual nature of the land around you. Sacred space can also perform the action of neutralizing or removing any energy in the prescribed area that is inimical or unsupportive of your intention.

Methods for establishing or declaring an area as sacred are commonly found in grimoires. Collecting them can be an interesting study in different methods, which may be used at various times in specific places or circumstances. Techniques for establishing sacred space can include drawing a circle with a stick or magical tool, sprinkling powdered herbs, burning dried herbs to create sacred smoke with which to bless an area, or misting the area with blessed water. Spoken words delivered with intention can also create sacred space.

Establishing sacred space often uses one or more of the four elements. Drawing on the energy of the elements is a common technique to consecrate or bless objects and places. For ideas about creating sacred space with herbs, water, and other things, see Chapter 6.

COMMON TOOLS, USES, AND ASSOCIATIONS

Information about tools is usually found in a grimoire. While the practice of green witchcraft isn't necessarily formal, there are tools that practitioners often use in their work, either practically or symbolically. Note that these are not the main four magical tools of the Western occult tradition (athame/knife, pentacle, wand, cup), although some are similar.

The following basic associations and uses are just that: basic. I encourage you to start with these and explore more via reading and research. Different cultures can assign different symbolism to these tools, and cultural myths can suggest different uses. Reading and research are how you take your practice to a different level, because you challenge yourself to expand your horizons and understanding of basic symbology.

Cup

The cup is traditionally seen as a feminine symbol, with receptive energy (as opposed to projective). It is associated with the element of water. The cup is associated with transformation, purification, and containment—but gentle containment, not restrictive. Think of a mother cradling a child in her arms and you'll have a sense of the energy the cup carries.

Cauldron

The cauldron carries many of the same energies that the cup does, as it, too, is a receptacle. However, the cauldron is a more active symbol. A cauldron is used to transform disparate energies and blend them into something unique and new. The cauldron is also associated with abundance and plenty, nourishment, and warmth.

Knife

The knife carries a projective energy. Single- or double-bladed, it is generally a tool that is considered practical in the practice of witchcraft, and it sees actual material use instead of symbolic use. You probably use it to chop up herbs, trim the ends of flower stalks, and so forth. Symbolically, think of the knife as a concentrated application of your will to change something.

Boline

The boline is a knife used to harvest. It has a curved blade and looks like a miniature sickle. In some witchcraft traditions, the athame is a dull blade, used symbolically only, which necessitates having a second bladed tool for cutting. The boline serves this purpose.

In practical terms, a boline isn't necessarily the tool you'd reach for while foraging or working in your garden. Sturdy scissors or secateurs would fill this role much better. And because much of green witchcraft is practical rather than ceremonial, your everyday gardening tool is probably imbued with the energy of tending to the cycle of nature as it manifests in your garden and therefore is an excellent symbol of caring for and harvesting plants.

Staff or Wand

The staff or wand is the sticklike tool often used to project or direct energy in traditional witchcraft. In green witchcraft, a staff is more likely to be a walking stick, used to help you make your way through woodland or scrub. A staff or wand can also represent the world tree, a concept found in many cultures, linking above with below.

Broom

A broom is a green witch mainstay. It represents hospitality, care for the home, and maintaining the balance of harmony. It can be a tool for purification, as well as a practical household item. It can also represent the world tree, as a staff can.

Candles and Oil Lamps

Light and flame represent spirit, insight, protection, and energy. We tend to think of candles as the default, but oil lamps are very safe when used as directed, and the flame is protected. Candles and other sources of flame can help you focus, signifying a change in awareness or a shift in vibration when they are lit. They can be foci for meditation or company during a vigil.

The symbolism of light in the dark is a powerful one, and you can use that symbolism in so many different ways. Think of some, and note them down in your grimoire.

Light of any kind is representative of flame. LED candles can symbolize fire, if you prefer.

CHAPTER 5
Adding the Magic of Plants to Your Grimoire

FOR GREEN WITCHES, PLANTS ARE A LARGE PART of their magical work, and they figure significantly in their spiritual practice. A green witch can never have too many new and interesting tidbits of information about plant magic. Personal interactions with plants yield observations about their energies; reading modern and historical sources about their uses can expand and inspire your practice and applications. Even if the information as written isn't something you can or want to include in your grimoire, it can spark ideas. Traditional practices, your own intuition, and how you interact with the energy of the plant all serve to direct you along your own path of discovery. Your grimoire is an important partner in that work.

Creating Herbal Entries

One of the central parts of your grimoire will be the information you collect about plants, trees, and flowers. How you set up this information will be important to your work as a green witch.

Recording this information should be done clearly, concisely, and with attribution to the source and/or reference. There's a lot of information to include too; noting down only magical correspondences is limiting the ways in which you can draw on a plant's energy. Let's look at the different sections of a proper entry.

The following order and information is applicable to trees, flowers, and herbs; we'll use the word *plant* to stand in for all of these here, but know that you can use this format for any type of flora you are trying to record.

1. **The name of the plant.** This is important in a variety of ways. First, include the botanical name, which never changes the way folk names can. Record common names, too (and yes, there are usually more than one), including outdated ones. There is more than one plant known as mandrake, for example.

2. **Physical description and traits.** Describe how the plant looks. You can use a photo, a botanical illustration, or a sample of the actual plant as your source. Include infor-

mation such as the shape of the leaf, stem, flowers, and/ or fruit.

3. **Illustration.** You can draw this yourself, trace a botanical illustration, or photocopy a photo from a book. If you use someone else's work as an inspiration or a mechanical copy, note down the source.

4. **Toxicity/warnings.** Note down any toxic warnings associated with the plant. This includes touching the leaves, juice, or sap; breathing in the scent; breathing in the smoke if burned; and ingesting the plant. Even if you don't plan to do these things with the plant, note them down anyway. This is critical information to include; make sure you write down the specifics.

5. **Geographic information.** What region of the world does the plant grow in? What kinds of environments? If you know the planting zone for it, include that information. Also note down the region or locale to which the plant is native. (This information becomes important when you focus on working with local and native plants, an important part of green witchcraft. See the discussion on local flora and working with local energies in Chapter 10.)

6. **Medical information.** Even if you don't intend to use the plant medicinally, write down this information; the knowledge is useful for rounding out your records. Note down what specific parts are used in particular treatments. You can draw on this information magically too; energy is energy, after all.

7. **Practical and historical uses.** This information may overlap with medicinal applications—for example, using lavender in strewing herbs to deter fleas, or cedar to repel moths.

8. **Traditional magical information.** What have past witches used this plant for? What are the magical uses that have become common in practice? What parts of the plant are used for specific purposes? Remember to note your sources for each bit of information.

9. **Your personal magical information.** This is just as important as traditional uses for the plant in question. Your experiences and interactions with it hold perhaps more weight than those of a practitioner a century ago. Record here your energy-sensing exercises, your experiences and interactions with the plant. Cross-reference this information with the results you record of your spells and magical workings involving the plant. (See the Sensing Energy exercise in Chapter 6.)

10. **Examples of the plant.** A pressed sample of the plant (leaves, flowers, or other) is good to include in your reference entry. Alternatively, a small glassine envelope of crumbled dried plant matter can be glued or taped in. (See the Collecting Samples and Pressing Samples activities later in this chapter.)

WARNING If you include plant matter or soil samples in your grimoire, you will not be able to travel across country borders with it. Customs have strict rules about plant matter crossing them, even if it's dried; the risk of introducing foreign strains of bacteria or pests in hibernation is too great. These sorts of things can destabilize entire agricultural economies in worst-case scenarios. Be respectful of this and don't try to cross borders with dried or fresh plant matter.

If this looks like a lot of information, you're right; it is. You want your grimoire to be as complete as possible in order to provide you with as much information as it can. The more complete the information is; the more knowledge you can draw from it. It will also help you in later exercises and reflections that will be introduced in later chapters.

PLANT ENTRY

NAME OF THE PLANT

....

PHYSICAL DESCRIPTION AND TRAITS

....

....

....

....

....

....

ILLUSTRATION

TOXICITY/WARNINGS

GEOGRAPHIC INFORMATION

MEDICAL INFORMATION

PRACTICAL AND HISTORICAL USES

....

....

....

....

....

....

TRADITIONAL MAGICAL INFORMATION

....

....

....

....

....

PERSONAL MAGICAL INFORMATION

....

....

....

....

....

EXAMPLES OF THE PLANT

Here's what a completed entry could look like:

RED CLOVER

NAME OF THE PLANT
Trifolium pratense

PHYSICAL DESCRIPTION AND TRAITS
Perennial with red multi-petaled ball-like blossoms, which average $^3/_4$" in diameter. Height of clover plant can be between 8 and 30 inches, but they tend to be around 1 foot tall. The pinkish-purple flowers bloom from late spring through early fall. Three-lobed leaves give it the name "trefoil." Leaves are $^1/_2$" to 1" long, with a paler green crescent shape on the outer half of the leaf. Part of the legume family. Grows with a deep taproot, so is used to control erosion.

ILLUSTRATION

TOXICITY/WARNINGS
Can thin blood; contraindicated with anticoagulants and blood thinners. Phytoestrogens might interact with birth control. Toxic if taken with methotrexate (a medication used to treat some cancers, severe psoriasis, and rheumatoid arthritis).

GEOGRAPHIC INFORMATION
Native to Europe, western Asia, northwest Africa; planted and naturalized in other continents such as North and South America. Grows wild in a variety of environments. Enjoys full sun and well-drained soil, but hardy enough to grow in a variety of climates and soil conditions.

MEDICAL INFORMATION
ANCIENT: syphilis, psoriasis, eczema, anxiety.
MODERN: stress relief, respiratory issues (e.g., asthma, bronchitis), digestive issues, helps soothe inflammation (e.g., arthritis), helps treat menopausal and menstrual symptoms (due to isoflavones, which function like phytoestrogens). Improves circulation. Source of calcium, magnesium, potassium, vitamin C.

PRACTICAL AND HISTORICAL USES
Mentioned by Pliny the Elder. Important element in the pollination cycle, as it is a favorite of such insects as bumblebees. Grown and used as fodder for livestock.

TRADITIONAL MAGICAL INFORMATION

Purification, cleanses/purifies energy. Three-lobed leaves link it to the power of three and trinity deity expressions (maiden, mother, crone; father, son, spirit). Spring, new beginnings. Prosperity. Clover is among the herbs sacred to faeries. Darker red clover can be associated with lust, recovering from a breakup, attracting new partners. Four-lobed leaves are associated with good fortune.

PERSONAL MAGICAL INFORMATION

Sweetness, joy. Add dried flowers to spring incense, Beltane incense. Red clover tea: 1–2 teaspoons dried flowers to 1 cup hot water, steep for up to 30 minutes.

EXAMPLES OF THE PLANT

REFERENCES

Let's take a moment to talk about references. Citations are incredibly important. You may feel the information itself that you find online or in a book is what matters, but knowing where it came from is essential. Attributing the source correctly is a form of respecting the material and the original author or researcher. Being able to track back and verify the source is valuable; if you ever end up sharing the information, being able to direct other people to it is critical.

A quick way of noting sources and references is to color-code them. Instead of writing an author and/or title or online URL beside every piece of information, make a colored dot that corresponds to a reference source. Elsewhere (after your master index is a good place), make a list of sources and place a dot in the color you chose to represent it next to it, or underline the source in that color. If you run out of colors, start the color sequence again using a different symbol, such as a star, a square, or a triangle.

Enriching Your Grimoire with Samples

Adding plant samples to your grimoire is valuable in two ways. You get hands-on experience with the plant, and your grimoire's energy will be affected by a bit of the plant matter being contained in it. (See the Pressing Samples activity that immediately follows this one for instructions on how to press your samples to include in your grimoire.)

COLLECTING SAMPLES

This activity allows you to interact with the flora of your local environment in service of your grimoire. It's an excellent way to get to know the plants of your immediate vicinity, which can carry stronger energy for you to draw on in magic than exotic herbs or flowers imported from other areas in the world. Lavender and mandrake may be listed in reference books as carrying certain energy, but if they don't grow near you, how is that energy going to operate in your magic? Ideally, working with the energies of your local environment will bring a more personal resonance to your workings.

The term for collecting or harvesting plants from the wild is *wildcrafting*. Here are the steps to do it:

- **Positively identify the plant before you harvest anything from it.** This is critical, because if you don't know the plant, you can't be certain it's nontoxic. Positive identification is also important in order to avoid harvesting something that is protected. Use a guide that focuses on your geographic area or use an identification app on your smartphone.

- **Survey the area carefully.** Will harvesting this plant impact anything else? Are there other examples of the plant, or is this the only one? If harvesting it would negatively impact anything, don't do it.

- **With respect, extend your sense to the plant and inquire if you may take a sample of it.** If you get any feeling that is not a clear yes, don't touch it. Give water to the plant as an offering even if it says no; respect its answer and thank it for considering your request.

- **Don't uproot the entire plant.** Carefully snip a branch or leaf off, cutting at a 45-degree angle about ¼" above a leaf node to encourage growth.

- **Sketch or photograph the plant.** Also make note of the environment it was found in, recording down other species of plant that are growing with it.

- **Keep the samples damp to keep them as fresh as possible until you can press them.** To keep them fresh, fold them into a lightly dampened light cloth or paper towel and slip it into a plastic bag.

- **Leave the area in a better condition than you found it.** Clean up any litter or detritus that doesn't belong.

Remember that if you intend to use your sample for identification or study later, make sure it is as complete as possible from root to tip.

As an alternative to physically harvesting a sample of the plant, you can photograph it (and then print it out at home if you have a physical grimoire or use the digital photo if you keep a digital grimoire), label it, and add it to the page recording the plant's information. Don't forget to write down where you found it and what date it was harvested on.

You can also use this collecting sample activity with local rocks. Researching what kind of geologic makeup your area has can lead you in very interesting directions as you experiment with the energy of local rocks.

PRESSING SAMPLES

Pressing a sample helps preserve it. An easy way to press plants is with newspaper. This can be hard to find these days, so you can use flyers or other kinds of paper as well; just have a clean piece of paper (such as blotting paper) in direct contact with the plant. (You can buy blotting paper at an art or craft store.) If you have access to a large amount of undyed construction paper or other such paper, that would be ideal too. For the cardboard, you can deconstruct a shipping box and cut pieces from it.

WHAT YOU NEED

- Your plant sample(s)
- Newspaper or blotting paper
- Pieces of corrugated cardboard, roughly 8" × 10"
- 1–2 large, heavy books
- Glue
- Card stock (8" × 10")
- Cotton swab or small paintbrush
- Waxed paper
- Label

WHAT TO DO

1. Lay your sample(s) out as flat as possible on one layer of newspaper (with a few sheets in the layer). Fold the other side over the sample or lay another few pieces of paper on top.

2. Lay a piece of cardboard on top. Try to use corrugated board, which allows air to circulate better than a solid piece.

3. Begin the next layer of newspaper and sample(s), alternating with pieces of cardboard. (Think of it as a layer cake or a lasagna!)

4. When you have folded all the samples into paper, lay a heavy book or two on top and make sure the stack is out of the way. Leave it to dry.

5. Check every couple of days to see how the drying process is going. If the newspaper starts to get damp, trade it for fresh paper. Drying can take a week for thinner, lighter plant matter, or longer if you're pressing something with a fleshy stalk or very thick leaves. The faster it dries, the better the color and overall condition will be.

6. Once the sample is dry, mount it by gluing it to a piece of card stock. Use a cotton swab or small paintbrush to paint the glue on in a very light layer to avoid blobs of glue. Put a piece of waxed paper over the sample and put a heavy book on top of it to help the glued sample dry flat. Remove when dry.

7. On a label, identify the plant by its botanical name, common name(s), the location in which you found it, the date it was collected on, and any other pertinent information you feel should be included. Glue the label to the corner of the card.

8. Insert the card into your grimoire, or begin a separate file of sample cards to supplement your plant records.

Nature-Based Art

One of the joys of creating your own grimoire is being able to decorate it however you like. Using ideas and material sourced from nature is a wonderful way to incorporate your magical and practical herbal knowledge into art to enhance your grimoire. You can also use these activities as central actions in a seasonal ritual, to create seasonal decor, and as spells. Be creative and let your inspiration guide you.

LEAF PRINTING ACTIVITY

Another way to incorporate the magic of plants into your grimoire is to use them to make art with which to decorate your grimoire. You can do this activity seasonally using plant materials available at the time, or design your art using the energies carried by the leaves to create a magical artwork with intention.

Use as many or as few different colors of paint as you like. Practice on one piece of paper first to get a feel for how much paint you'll need to use for the plant matter you've chosen.

WHAT YOU NEED
- Leaves (or flower petals, twigs, or other plant matter)
- Paint (colors your choice)
- Shallow tray or plate
- Paintbrush
- Paper
- Cup of water to wash brush
- Paper towel

WHAT TO DO

1. Sort through the plant matter and remove any pollen, dirt, or stamens. Look for matter that will press flat on your paper.

2. Pour small amounts of the paint on your tray or plate.

3. Use the paintbrush to apply paint to one side of the plant matter. Don't apply it too thickly, or the resulting print will lose detail, and the risk of smudging will increase.

4. Press the plant paint side down onto a piece of paper and lift it away carefully. Try to do it as straight up and down as you can to eliminate smudging. A silhouette of the leaf, petal, or twig should be left on your paper.

5. Continue, cleaning the brush when you switch colors. If there is paint left on the plant matter, press it onto a scrap piece of paper until it leaves no print, then apply the new color of paint. If your chosen matter is highly textured, try dampening a piece of paper towel and pressing it onto that to help remove paint from the textured areas.

6. Allow your prints to dry. Cut them out and glue them into your grimoire wherever you choose.

NATURE ART ACTIVITY

Making pictures out of natural materials is a lovely way to connect with your immediate natural environment, and the bonus is that you can use it to decorate your grimoire. This is also a lovely way to engage in spellwork, creating an image or pattern with intent.

WHAT YOU NEED
- Elements found in nature (see instructions)
- Heavy paper or card stock/pasteboard
- Glue
- Small paintbrush
- Page protector (optional)

WHAT TO DO
1. Wander through your chosen natural area. This could be an arboretum, a lakeside, a park, or your own backyard.

2. Collect bits of things that catch your attention. Leaves, flowers, grass, fallen pieces of bark, and stone chips can all be used, among other things. Try to avoid thick or heavy things; they will be challenging to incorporate into your art, and difficult to fasten into the grimoire.

3. Once home, take a piece of heavy paper or pasteboard cut to your desired size (take into account the size of your grimoire pages), and arrange your found objects to make a pattern, image, or shape. When you are happy with it, lift each piece carefully one by one and apply glue to the back with the paintbrush. Set it down on the paper in

its place again. Carry on working through all the found objects in your art like this.

4. Allow the artwork to dry. If you like, you can add hand-drawn elements to your artwork.

5. When it is finished, glue it into your grimoire. If you are worried that the objects will separate from the backing, slip it into a page protector sheet and glue that into your grimoire. If your art is smaller than a standard page protector, trim the extra parts of the page protector and tape it closed, then attach the smaller protected artwork into the grimoire.

TIP If you want to use plant matter that is not dry, look up how to dry it in the previous Pressing Samples activity. Proceed with this activity once the plant matter is ready.

STAMPING ACTIVITY

This is another relaxing activity that can make art for your grimoire out of plants. If you use an apple, you can slice it widthwise to reveal the seeds around the core and use it as a stamp without any further work. Select the fruit or vegetable you use for its magical energies, if you like, to create art for a spell's goal.

WHAT YOU NEED

- Carrot, potato, and/or apple (or other fruits or vegetables of your choice)
- Kitchen knife
- Cutting board
- Paper towel
- Paint (colors your choice)
- Tray or plate
- Paper

WHAT TO DO

1. Wash and dry your chosen fruits or vegetables.

2. Using the knife and cutting board, slice each fruit or vegetable in half. You can leave them like this, or slice them again to make thick slices. You can then use the knife to cut the slices into shapes, such as stars, crescents, or whatever you like.

3. Pat the open slices dry with the paper towel.

4. Pour small puddles of paint onto the tray or plate. Don't go overboard; you can add more later.

5. Choose a plant stamp and dip it into one of the puddles of paint. Lift it and place it on your paper. Lift the shape straight up, leaving a print on the paper.

6. Continue, alternating stamps and colors as you choose. Wipe the paint off the stamp before dipping it into a different color.

7. When the stamped papers are dry, you can use them as divider pages or endpapers in your grimoire, or as paper for spells. If you use recycled paper and substitute nature-based dyes for the paint—crushed berries, beet juice, and the like—you can also use them as offerings outdoors.

PART 2

Using Your Green Witch Grimoire

A GREEN WITCH'S GRIMOIRE isn't meant to sit on a shelf. It's meant to be used often, thumbed through, written in, scribbled on, and consulted. It's the place to record ideas and new information, and keep track of your spellwork and rituals. It's where you collect information about spell materials, store things that inspire you, and journal your meditations and reflections. It's a collection of memories and dreams, goals, and obstacles. In other words, the grimoire is the reflection of your spiritual journey, which means that it, too, is always in development. It's a symbol of your path and your direction, which shifts as your growth takes place.

This part will look at what you can do with your grimoire, expanding on some of the ideas in Part 1 and introducing new ones. The grimoire becomes a symbol, but it also becomes a spiritual guide, allowing you to delve into your own spiritual growth and explore your evolution as a green witch. It offers you the chance to gain insight into your ethical system and to shine a light on the morals you value, and it offers you the knowledge about yourself that can enable you to serve nature out in the physical world.

CHAPTER 6

Practicing Witchcraft with Your Grimoire

YOUR GRIMOIRE IS YOUR COMPANION as you explore your spiritual path. It's a partner and a mirror, where you can look to trace your development and gain insight, record spells and rituals, and collect lore and personal reflections. In this chapter you will explore how the grimoire functions in your craft, including being a resource for basic techniques, a participant in activities and exercises, an asset that both informs and interprets divination, and a body of research and wisdom to be consulted.

Using the Grimoire to Explore and Deepen Your Connection to Spirit

Any magical tool you use regularly will begin to absorb energy and gradually take on its own character, its own energy personality. The grimoire is no exception. Of particular interest is your use of it as a magical journal to record meditations, to hold your steam-of-consciousness responses to rituals or spells, and the like. Your grimoire is the record of your spiritual journey but also a tool to help further your development. By reviewing its records of your past activities and musings, you can use it as a sort of window to your past self.

You can also use your grimoire as a power sink, where you empower it with extra energy every time you use it or when you've finished a working and have leftover energy. Think of it as grounding into the grimoire instead of the earth after ritual, spellwork, or meditation.

Basic Green Witch Techniques

An overview of basic techniques is usually part of a grimoire. No matter what stage of your journey you're at, reframing basics is a good exercise because it forces you to break them down to the simplest ideas and concepts. This is a good thing to do on a regular basis, because as you develop and advance, you'll be able to interpret the basic techniques in a different light.

Let's do a brief review of some techniques you should be able to use as a green witch. These aren't detailed step-by-step instructions; they're descriptions of the techniques. For more detailed explorations of these techniques, explore the exercises in *The Green Witch*.

CENTERING AND GROUNDING

Centering and grounding is a foundational technique that forms the core of most other energy work you'll do as a green witch. In essence, you find your personal energy center, then reach out for that to connect with the earth's energy. Like a root, it stabilizes you, and can also serve as a method to rebalance your energy, whether you have too much or too little. You may use a familiar form of centering and grounding, but note down or copy out new versions and ideas of the technique as you come across them. Experiment with imagery, motion, and other aspects, and journal your experiences.

SENSING ENERGY

Sensing energy is a step beyond centering and grounding. Visualize reaching out with a tendril of your energy, the way you did to seek and connect to the earth's energy. Instead of immersing it in another energy source, however, allow it to brush the surface of something, either object or area. Allow that touch to serve as your connection to what you're trying to gather information on, keeping your mind open to intuitive jumps and alerts.

Like with centering and grounding, you may already have a familiar technique for this, but record new ones as you find them. Likewise, record your experiences and impressions when practicing energy sensing. And practice it a lot. Every reading you do of an item's energy is valuable for that personal interaction: Traditional associations may be traditional, but your personal experience with it and your interpretation of its energy are what is really important. These are the critical pieces of information to record in your grimoire, as they create the unique body of knowledge that serves as the foundation for an authentic practice.

> **WARNING** Thoroughly research the item whose energy you plan to read before you engage with it to determine any toxicity. If you have allergies, sensitivities, or pulmonary problems, leave out the steps that may harm you.

SENSING ENERGY

Here is an exercise to practice your skills at energy sensing. As it involves using the four elements, modify the exercise as necessary according to the object you're working with. For example, a piece of jewelry can't be crumbled or bruised, and a book or card can't be exposed to water. This is a good exercise to practice with plant matter; try a fresh and dried sample of whatever herb you're working with and note down the differences.

WHAT YOU NEED
- Item to be sensed
- Grimoire (or pertinent section of your grimoire)
- Writing tool
- Charcoal censer
- Lighter or matches
- Small dish of water

WHAT TO DO
1. Hold your hands over the item to be sensed. Extend your awareness. What sort of things do you pick up? Is there a physical sensation in your hands? Do ideas or feelings come to mind? Note down your observations in your grimoire.

2. Touch and/or hold the object. Extend your senses. What do you sense? Note down your observations in your grimoire.

3. Physically alter a bit of the object. Crumble or bruise a bit of it in your hands. How does the energy change? Try

burning a pinch on a charcoal censer. Touch the smoke with your fingers and hold your hands over the smoke. What do you sense? Waft a bit of the smoke toward you carefully. What does the smell evoke? Note down your observations in your grimoire.

4. Put a pinch or torn bit of it in the dish of water. Does the wet change the energy in any way? Note down your observations in your grimoire.

5. Review your notes and write a summary of the experience.

MEDITATION

Basic meditation techniques are good to have in your green witch tool kit. You'll find that altering your state via meditation will help put you in a mindset more conducive to intuitive work. In essence, meditation can support a mindful awareness, which is the state you're striving for in much of your work as a green witch. Basic meditation can be as simple as relaxing your body and breathing deeply for a set number of inhalations.

When you discover a new technique that works well for you, write it in your grimoire. Experiment with focusing on different concepts, images, or objects as you meditate, and note down your experiences. After a meditation session, always take a few minutes to write a sentence or two about your experience: why you decided to meditate, what your state of mind was before you began and what it was afterward, and any particularly noteworthy observations about your session.

Writing responses to guided meditations is also very important. A guided meditation is a meditation in a story-like setting, usually recorded or led by someone else. You listen to the story or description and follow the directions the speaker gives. For example, a guided meditation might lead you to spiritually meet the spirit of a plant or tree, and allow you to converse with it. It's an excellent way to deepen your spiritual practice and explore various themes you feel are important.

Sacred Space

Having a set routine or set of actions to create sacred space is fine, and that's something you'll want to write into your grimoire. There are other ways to involve your grimoire's contents in designing new ways to create sacred space, however. You might choose an alternative method for a specific purpose, for example, to pair a new way of creating sacred space with the goal of your intended working. Here are some techniques for creating sacred space that you can include in your grimoire as you construct it. Use them as is, as templates, or as inspiration for completely different methods that you create on your own.

SACRED SPACE: DECLARATION
Center yourself and calm your body and focus by taking three slow deep breaths. After your third exhalation, say:

Spirits of Nature, I honor and respect you.
I acknowledge the divine in Nature and ask that it
bless me.
I declare this space sacred and appropriate for my
purpose.
So may it be; so it is.

SACRED SPACE: SMOKE CLEANSING

Various cultures use the method of blessing or consecrating an area with smoke. North American indigenous peoples call it *smudging*; a northern European tradition (Anglo-Saxon, Old English) is known as using *recels*; a Gaelic word for blessing with smoke is *saining*. Hoodoo has a version where smoke from sacred herbs is lifted with the hands and "washed" over the body. If you use incense, it's only a step further to approach cleansing or blessing with smoke. Essentially, either dried herbs are sprinkled on charcoal, or dried stalks are wrapped together with a natural fiber and lit, the flame then blown out and the end allowed to smolder, producing smoke.

Burning things releases energy; it's why spells use the method of burning things written on a piece of paper. Burning also releases energy in the form of light and heat created by the fuel. In the case of plant matter, the energies associated with the herbs in your blend are released.

Here are some good plants to use in smoke cleansing and blessings:

- **Vervain:** Used for protection, purification, and clearing negative energy. Vervain is also used for healing and to attract good fortune.

- **Mugwort:** This herb clears energies, leaving a blank slate. It also has a clearing effect on the mind and a heightening of the extra senses, so it is a good thing to start any working that is going to involve an altered or trance state at some point.

- **Lavender:** A calming herb, lavender is used for health, divination, relaxation, and psychic development. Grind the dried flowers to sprinkle on a charcoal censer, or use the stalks with leaves to bundle into a stick shape.

- **Sage:** White sage is becoming problematic in terms of ethical consumption and cultural appropriation. A perfectly useful alternative is garden sage (*Salvia officinalis*), which grows well in a garden, in a window box, or as a windowsill herb. Sage is associated with purification and wisdom.

- **Rosemary:** Rosemary is commonly used to protect, ward off negative energy, purify, and bless. Use a fresh sprig to dip into water to sprinkle, or ground dried rosemary to burn on charcoal.

MAKE AN HERBAL BLESSING WAND

Incense is one way to use the energy of plant matter to affect the energy of a person, an object, or a place. A blessing wand is a different way to use fire and air to transform plant matter. You are probably familiar with the smudge stick used by some Native American tribes; this is a similar principle. Choose your herb stalks to reflect your desired goals. For example, lavender is associated with purification energy, sage is associated with wisdom, and rosemary is associated with health. This combo could be used for cleansing a sickroom and blessing upcoming surgery or mental health maintenance.

WHAT YOU NEED
- Dried herb stalks (suggestions include rosemary, sage, or lavender)
- Natural-fiber string
- Small dish of sand

WHAT TO DO
1. Take stems, leaves, and/or stalks of dried herbs and lay them on top of one another. Trim the ends so they are roughly even.

2. With a natural-fiber string, tie the bundle firmly at the top, the middle, and the bottom, snipping off the string after each tie.

3. Lay out the remaining length of string in a horizontal line on your work surface. Place the bundle on top of the string's midpoint and tie the string around the bottom firmly. Wrap the ends of the string up the bundle in a crisscross fashion, tying it where the string crosses over itself if you like, and tie it securely when you've reached the top.

4. To use, hold the top to a flame so the dried material catches fire. Wave the bundle gently to put out the flame, but blow on it gently to encourage the embers to continue

glowing and producing smoke. Use your other hand to waft the smoke around the area to be consecrated.

5. To extinguish the bundle, place it smoldering-end down into a small dish of sand. Make sure it has extinguished completely and is cold before wrapping the bundle in foil to store it until the next time you need it.

MAKE A LAVENDER BLESSING WAND

Lavender stalks dry very well and, when bound together, make an excellent wand for smoke blessings. Lavender resonates with gentle peace and purification, and it is a good all-purpose herb for household use.

WHAT YOU NEED
- Dried lavender stalks
- Natural-fiber string or raffia
- Small dish of sand

WHAT TO DO
1. As lavender flowers grow at the top of the stalk, take several stalks and lay a few down, then place the next few so that their flowers are farther down the stalk of the first ones, overlapping the first round. Repeat these steps with more stalks. Essentially you're making a line of flowers parallel with the first stalks laid down.

2. Take a small amount of natural-fiber string (or raffia) and tie the bundle together near the top, around the middle, and just below the last flowers, snipping the string after each tie.

3. Lay the remaining length of string out in a horizontal line and lay the bundle on the string's midpoint, on top of the last tie at the bottom. Tie the string securely around the bundle, then wrap the bundle in a crisscross pattern all the way to the top. Tie off the string again. If you like, you can tie the string each time it crosses over itself for added security. You want the bundle to be tight and to be secure enough to not fall apart when the wraps begin to burn away as the bundle smolders.

4. To use, hold the top to a flame so the dried material catches fire. Wave the bundle gently to put out the flame, but blow on it gently to encourage the embers to continue glowing and producing smoke. Use your other hand to waft the smoke around the area to be consecrated.

5. To extinguish the bundle, place it smoldering end down into a small dish of sand. Make sure it has extinguished completely and is cold before wrapping the bundle in foil to store it until the next time you need it.

SACRED SPACE: STREWING HERBS

Another way to use herbs to bless a space is by strewing them, or scattering them around on the ground. You can use dried or fresh herbs; either way, make sure they are chopped or ground for easier dispersal. While just tossing herbs on the ground would be a passive way to add their energy to a space, it's more efficient to charge them first.

> To charge something means to program it with a specific intent, usually done by invoking the specific energy you wish to use to activate, or by holding the herbs in your hands and infusing them with the desired energy before using them. As you experiment with various techniques for charging objects or materials, add your favorites to your grimoire.

Sprinkle the herbs with intent. Leave them for a period of time, then sweep them up with thanks for their energies. How long you leave them depends on the energy of the room you're trying to affect. If it's part of your weekly or monthly house-cleaning, an hour should do it. If you're trying to clear a room in a new home to remove or neutralize the energy left by previous tenants, leaving them overnight is a good idea. Compost the herbs after sweeping them up.

SACRED SPACE: ASPERGING

Asperging is the act of sprinkling something with blessed water to consecrate it. The easiest way to do this is to bless a cup or bowl of water, then dip your fingers in and sprinkle drops off the tips by flicking your hand. Blessing water can be as simple as holding your hands over it and charging it with your intent, bathing the water with energy charged with blessing. In this case, your intent would be to consecrate or bless something. (For more information on blessing and charging things, see *The Green Witch*.)

Asperging can also unite water and earth. Steep dried or fresh herbs in water for at least 3 hours, then strain. Use this water to asperge the space. Or you can use blessed water and dip stalks of fresh herbal matter into it, and shake droplets off the herb. Rosemary is particularly good for this. If you don't grow your own herbs or have only dried, you can often buy stalks of fresh herbs in the produce section of supermarkets. Other good herbs to use for asperging are fresh lavender or sage stalks. Dip a stalk of your chosen herb into the water and use it to sprinkle drops around your chosen space.

CHAPTER 7

Using Your Grimoire in Energy and Spellwork

YOUR GRIMOIRE IS PART MANUAL, part reference book, and part lab notebook. As you work with it, it will collect and expand in parallel with your practice, reflecting your growth and insight.

Interacting with your grimoire is a skill that may feel awkward at first but will grow easier the more you use it. Part of this is due to the accrual of information in it, but part is also due to the energy relationship that you build with it. Like any other tool, the grimoire becomes imprinted with your energy when you use it, whether that be by reading it, adding information to it, or doing ritual or spellcraft with it. And the more energy it accumulates, the more successful it will become at supporting you and your goals.

Part of the energy it accumulates comes from your act of recording your spellwork, rituals, and other spiritual and magical activity. But your grimoire can be part of that magic itself as well. This chapter explores how it can function as a magical tool in your practice.

Divination in Green Witch Practice

Divination is a mode of communication with the energy at large in your environment, as well as your subconscious. It's a way to link the two for dialogue, through which you can gain valuable insight about the world and your own subconscious.

Divination is a useful practice to help you hone your intuition, as well as refine your own understanding of the energies of the plants, stones, trees, and other natural elements at your fingertips. By working with them, you can build up a reference system based on your own interpretations and interactions with materials.

THE GRIMOIRE IN DIVINATION

The grimoire can be a very useful tool in divination. It is a record of your impressions and personal experiences with various natural and spiritual energies. This record becomes your reference for the omens and signs you encounter.

Apart from this, the grimoire becomes a body of work that is greater than the sum of its parts. By recording both physical or material information (about clover, for example) as well as spiritual or magical information, you strengthen the multilayered aspect of the universe, reinforcing that information and valuable insight come from everywhere. Collecting that body of knowledge, combined with your personal experiences and opinions, gives you the correspondences and insight to see deeper into signs, omens, and symbolic activity. As you work with divination, you will begin to understand that each tree, number, deity, animal, bird, color, stone, star, herb, or human principle is associated with symbols in your personal system. The object of recording your divination study and readings is to amass this information as you discover it. Repeatedly recognizing omens or signs will eventually bring about subconscious associations. This will start to become available to you in everyday life, providing intuitive wisdom.

BRIEF OVERVIEW OF COMMON DIVINATION METHODS

The tarot card system is probably the most familiar form of divination. This isn't the place to go into it, but if the organized system of symbols and such appeals to you, I encourage you to find a deck with art that speaks to you and begin your study of it. Use your journal to write down your impressions as you study the cards (meditating on them one at a time is a great way to explore them), and keep that information as part of your grimoire. Your personal responses to the cards are valuable, possibly more so than traditional meanings associated with a specific card.

What may interest green witches more, however, are the various oracle decks that exist. Oracle decks have a varying number of cards with different images on them that generally come with a booklet outlining what each card is meant to represent, according to the artist or creator of the deck. Like with tarot decks, you can find an oracle deck on almost any subject (I have botanical sets, a bird set, a fiber arts set, and so forth). Just like with a tarot deck, forging a new relationship with a new oracle deck by meditating on each card and writing down your feelings and interpretations of each card can be of more use to you and your grimoire than relying solely on the artist's or designer's intent.

The pendulum is another divination tool favored by intuitive witches like those on the green path. A quotation popularly attributed to Albert Einstein, who had an interest in dowsing, states, "The dowsing rod is a simple instrument which shows the reaction of the human nervous system to certain factors which are unknown to us at this time." Like the dowsing rod, the pendulum is an object that responds to minuscule movements initiated by the nervous system, prompted by the body reacting to messages coming from the energy around it. Pendulums can be made from crystals, wood, or metals, or can be as simple as any sort of weight hanging from a string. The art of using a pendulum lies mainly in knowing what kind of questions to ask to help gain insight.

Other intuitive methods you could explore are scrying in water and scrying in a candle flame. Both ask you to use the item as a visual focus to allow your mind to disconnect from the physical world and be open to images, ideas, and visions; this device is referred to as a speculum. For example, the archetypical crystal ball is a scrying tool; black mirrors are also popular. Bowls of water or ink, polished stones, and even candle flames are all used as a visual focus in order to shift consciousness to receive impressions regarding a problem or situation. All these specula serve as a visual focus to occupy the conscious mind while the subconscious mind becomes active. A relaxed, dreamy state enables us to perceive more than we do when we think we are alert and conscious of our environment. When we are "alert" in this way, we are in fact focusing a little too hard on the world around us. When relaxed, we are more likely to trust our intuition, which is what divination is all about.

Far and away, the most green witch–adjacent system of divination, however, is the interpretation of omens and occurrences in everyday life to uncover the messages carried therein.

OMENS AND MESSAGES IN DAILY LIFE

Being in harmony with your environment means being able to pick up messages from it, whether those messages be overt or very quiet. When you encounter images or mentions of things or ideas that are associated with your practice of green witchcraft, they may catch your attention. Note them down, and when you are with your grimoire, look through the related area for information on the element that caught your attention.

Remember, though, that this depends on the mention being in a context in which you wouldn't normally find it. If you're walking through a greenhouse, for example, seeing roses or overhearing people talking about them is absolutely normal. Reading a cookbook and coming across a mention of sage as a particularly appropriate seasoning for a dish is common. However, if you're reading news headlines and come across a mention of rosemary, that's unlikely enough that you might want to take note of it and consider what message it has for you. Look up rosemary in your grimoire and read about its physical or medical uses, as well as its magical associations and whatever other information you may have collected. Is there anything that leaps out at you? What information strikes you as having meaning for you today?

Intuition is one of the key elements in divination, especially in a free-form system such as green witchcraft and reading your everyday life for guidance. If something catches your notice, be in the moment and take it in. Then consider why it caught your attention. Note it down as soon as you can, even on a scrap of paper or in the notepad app of your smartphone. Don't rely on your memory to recall all the subtleties and complexities hours later when you actually reach your grimoire to write about it. (Write about it hours later, by all means, but use those notes to prompt your memory to recall more detail than it would otherwise.)

RECORDING DIVINATIONS

Part of building a reference for divination in your grimoire is keeping track of what you've seen or encountered. Whether you've chosen to keep a separate book of your divination experiences or you have a section marked in your grimoire for that use, keeping track of your experiences is important. First, it reinforces that you are open to receiving messages. This encourages your subconscious to be more alert to noticing things, which in turn improves your ability to pick up messages. Second, the act of recording an experience moves it to another level of your mind. It engages with your conscious analytical brain, which allows you to turn the idea over in your mind and free-associate with it, thinking about it on a different level instead of simply allowing the intuition to prompt you vaguely.

So how do you record divinatory experiences like this? First, create a reliable sequence of actions that will signal to your subconscious what frame of mind it's expected to be in: relaxed, clear, and open. An easy sequence could be washing your hands and face, settling down in a customary spot, closing your eyes, and taking nine deep breaths while holding your divination tool in your hands. Using a regular set sequence will accelerate the process of getting into that frame of mind, like a shortcut. After using this sequence for a while, you'll find that accessing meaning and receiving enlightenment and insight will come more freely. As with anything else, practice makes you better at what you're practicing.

RECORDING DIVINATION

Like with any other regular activity, setting up a ritualized sequence of actions will help you create an easily achieved frame of mind for recording your divinatory experiences and reflecting on them. Optimizing that setting will allow you to access the most from your experience. You should choose a particular incense and candle that you reserve just for recording divinations. Lighting, smelling, and seeing these items will be part of the shortcut to creating your mental setting.

WHAT YOU NEED

- Incense and censer
- Matches or lighter
- Candle and candleholder
- Grimoire (or the divination notebook/section of your collected grimoire)
- Preferred writing implement

WHAT TO DO

1. Center and ground (see Chapter 6).

2. Light the incense.

3. Light the candle.

4. Open the grimoire or divination journal to a new page and take up your pen or pencil.

5. Take a few moments to close your eyes and think about the omen or sign you encountered.

6. Open your eyes and begin to write. Note down where and when you encountered the omen and in what form. (Did you see it in real life? Did you come across a mention of it in a podcast or article and it spoke to you somehow? Did you pass someone on the street and overhear a word from their phone conversation? Did you dream about it?)

7. Write down what it made you think of and how it made you feel.

8. Have you encountered this omen before? If so, what associations did it hold that time? Compare it to this experience.

9. Look up the omen in reference books, beginning with your own grimoire. Have you collected information on the symbol previous to this? If not, note associations and connections down in this divination portion of your grimoire, and transfer them to your reference section later.

RECORD AND REVIEW DIVINATION

Make a habit of reading through your divination records every so often to see if you have any new insight to add or connections to make. Often, your subconscious mind does work behind the scenes, and a regular review of your material will provide opportunity for those connections or insights to come to the surface. Note those new connections down with the date so you know they were added later.

DIVINATION RECORD

Information to include in recording divinations:

DATE

....

LOCATION OF SIGHTING/OMEN/DIVINATION

....

METHOD USED

....

WEATHER

....

MOON PHASE

....

YOUR HEALTH

....

THE OMEN OBSERVED/RECORD OF LAYOUT,
READING, OR OTHER ACTIVITY

....

....

....

INITIAL RESPONSE (AT THE TIME)

RESPONSE AFTER RESEARCH/REFLECTION

RESEARCH NOTES ASSOCIATED WITH SYMBOLS

LATER NOTES

Here's an example of a quick divination I did at the beginning of 2020.

READING FOR INSIGHT INTO THE UPCOMING YEAR, SPECIFICALLY RE. AS'S CAREER

DATE
4 January 2020

LOCATION OF SIGHTING/OMEN/DIVINATION
My study area

METHOD USED
Unraveled oracle deck

WEATHER
clear, cold

MOON PHASE
waxing (two days past first quarter)

YOUR HEALTH
tired; sleeping poorly; slow recovery from the Christmas trip

THE OMEN OBSERVED/RECORD OF LAYOUT, READING, OR OTHER ACTIVITY

Single card draw. Card pulled: Imagination (image: hand-knit socks: a complementary pair, but not identical. One is knit in yellow, gray, and pink like a pencil; the other is white with blue lines, like lined paper.).

INITIAL RESPONSE (AT THE TIME)

Things may not look like they work, but they fit together. Change your definition of matching/what succeeds. What is expected by most may not be what will work for you.

RESPONSE AFTER RESEARCH/REFLECTION

Booklet: "Magick. Intention. Go beyond what the eye can see. Anything is possible."

My intuition: Success comes in different forms; don't get trapped by what you hope for, or by what others expect of you. Change the goalposts. If anything is possible, then let's take this big step and give this different life setup a try.

RESEARCH NOTES ASSOCIATED WITH SYMBOLS

A pair doesn't mean two identical objects. Think of a pair of people; two different people entirely, who work well together. Mainstream isn't for everybody. What society expects of an adult's career isn't necessarily the life path for everyone.

LATER NOTES

Mid-February 2020:

Wow, the gamble is paying off so far, two months into the new setup. Everyone is happier, and it looks like there's more good stuff coming down the line.

Addendum:

My own health problems mean I need to internalize the advice from this divination as well. I need to redefine my own concept of success in light of the limitation of my chronic illness, and not feel guilty about it.

Spellcraft and Green Witchcraft

Spellcraft is entwined with the green witch practice. At its heart, spellcraft is moving energy with the goal of healing or rebalancing energy that is out of harmony. Restoring balance is a green witch's main pursuit, usually taking form in healing, managing energies, and being in harmony with the surrounding area.

If you are an intuitive practitioner, you may not do a lot of planning for your spellwork. That isn't necessarily a problem. What you may find difficult is the sitting down and recording of your activity once you've finished casting or whatever working you've engaged in. It's at odds with intuitive, spontaneous activity, and it can be a challenge to get yourself into the habit of doing it. Recording your work is important, however. It's good self-discipline, and it's also a good exercise to look at your intuitive decisions and figure out why you made them.

When recording activity or workings, always leave space for later reflections and feedback. And then, use it! Go through your records regularly and think about the work you did, how the situation seems to have responded to the working, and how you feel about it. This kind of reflection is part of what keeping records is for, and what makes your grimoire so valuable. Going back to consult a past activity and thinking about how it may have impacted future events is how you build your own aggregate of correspondences and important knowledge about your own practice. It can also become the basis for fine-tuning your practice, as well as offering you a valuable glimpse into your own direction and development.

RECORDING SPELLS

In order for a record to be of as much use in the future as possible, include as much information as you can, starting from the vague concept you have for your spell. Keep track of the brainstorming, the idle musings, and the rejected ideas. Write down everything you plan to do, the words, the gestures, the supplies, and the when and where. And then, once you've performed the spell, record how you deviated from your plan, and your immediate reaction to the casting. All this information can be helpful in analyzing the results at a later date.

Consider having a separate section in your grimoire for spells that have proven useful or particularly successful so you can reuse them.

SPELL RECORD

1. PLANNING

Object/goal/purpose:

....

....

Key words:

....

....

Ideas:

....

....

Supplies/symbols to use:

....

....

Tools:

....

....

Central symbolic action:

....

....

2. **WRITE OUT THE SPELL**

Include statement of intent:

....

....

....

....

....

3. **PERFORM THE SPELL**

4. **RECORD THE SPELL**

Date/time/place:

....

Additional desired info (weather, moon phase/sign, and so on):

....

Immediate report (how it felt, how it went, and so on):

....

....

....

Any changes:

....

....

....

ADD NOTES REGARDING CHANGES OR FUTURE IDEAS

....

....

....

....

....

....

....

LEAVE SPACE FOR NOTES WHEN REVIEWING SPELL

....

....

....

....

....

....

....

....

....

....

....

....

....

....

....

Here is an example of a spell record:

SPELL RECORD

1. PLANNING

Object/goal/purpose:

Healing for B's dog and newborn puppies; mastitis

Key words:

Reduce inflammation in mammary gland, reduce pain; maximize nutrition and weight gain of pups

Ideas:

Symbolism of opening a choked channel, ice

Supplies/symbols to use:

large/wide straw; milk; eyedropper; ice cube; bowl or glass

Tools:

none

Central symbolic action:

Pinch straw halfway down; drip milk into it with eyedropper; release pinch, allowing milk to flow into bowl; add ice cube to bowl of milk

2. WRITE OUT THE SPELL

Include statement of intent:

I work to support the health of Q and her pups, to clear her mastitis, allowing the inflamed gland to deliver milk, and for the pups to receive adequate nutrition.

3. PERFORM THE SPELL

4. RECORD THE SPELL

Date/time/place:

4 Feb 2020, 8:45 p.m., family altar

Additional desired info (weather, moon phase/sign, and so on):

overcast; waxing gibbous moon

Immediate report (how it felt, how it went, and so on):

Feels smooth, like adding to a flow; other people in the group are probably working, too, and group mind means we mesh well

Any changes:

Spilled milk, lol; I choose to see it as a reflection of how fruitful the bitch will be once her infection clears.

ADD NOTES REGARDING CHANGES OR FUTURE IDEAS

This is a good basic set of visualizations/symbolic actions for reducing fever and nourishing an ill body. Milk can represent any kind of nourishment. Could be tweaked to use chicken broth, or tea with honey, to reflect different kinds of illness?

LEAVE SPACE FOR NOTES WHEN REVIEWING SPELL

Immediate:
B says Q had surgery to remove the infected gland.

Review 1 week later:
B says everything is much better, quick recovery, and all the pups are gaining weight!

REVIEWING SPELLWORK

Casting an actual spell is important. Reviewing it is almost as important to your growth and development. If you don't analyze your success or failure, you're missing out on a lot of value of the experience. Tracing evolution is important to understand the roots of your current path and the direction you can go next.

Reviewing your spellwork is also a step toward supporting your experimentation. Asking yourself what could have been done differently is a good exercise. How could you have further refined the intent for a more precise target? What didn't feel quite right? What aspect of the spell worked really well and could be added to your toolbox of spell elements to be used at a later date in a different spell?

In addition, reviewing your spell records allows you to gain insight into your personal rhythms and energy use. Pay attention to the information about time of day, weather, moon phases, and so forth, and compare that data among a number of spells. Do you seem to have more success when you work during a particular phase of the moon? Do humid, overcast days put a damper on your magic? Being able to analyze your data means you can make your magical work more precise and efficient in the future.

You can also see how your needs have evolved. What topics or areas do you tend to work magic in most often? Break that down quarterly, looking at blocks of three months at a time to get a sense of how your spellwork shifts over a year's time, then extend it to two years, then more. Do you see an overall shift that reflects your life changes over those months and years? Do you see a pattern that correlates to the seasons, perhaps? All these kinds of data offer you insight into your own rhythms and responses to the events in your life. Deeper knowledge of yourself, your strengths, and your weaknesses can only help you in the future.

This knowledge can be used when analyzing ritual data, too, especially if you tend to do ritual more than spellwork. What you celebrate is also indicative of how you respond to your life changes, obstacles, and successes. This kind of insight is valuable in helping you fine-tune your future energy work, spellcraft, and rituals.

Intuitive Spellcraft: Using Your Grimoire to Guide You

Intuitive spellcraft is the technique of using your intuition to guide your actions and energy manipulation toward a goal. Bibliomancy—generally used as a form of divination—is an interesting method for intuitive spellcraft as well. Bibliomancy is the art of using a book to direct your next action. Simply put, you keep your goal or question in mind and then open the book randomly. The first thing you see and read on the page has some sort of connection to your situation and thus provides insight or reflection.

To use this technique in intuitive spellcraft, keep your goal or situation in mind and open your grimoire randomly. Take note of what is on the pages and jot down key words or points on a piece of paper. Use these ideas alone, or do the random opening of the book two more times. (Alternatively, you can open it as many times as you feel moved to, then study the notes you took for a theme or common thread that connects them.)

Look at the key words and ideas you noted down and combine them somehow to shape your spell. It may be using the words to speak magic, or assembling physical materials if the pages that fell open were reference lists of plants, or drawing on the spiritual energy of the materials or ideas as you move energy toward your goal.

Recording Rituals

Rituals are celebrations, as opposed to spells, which are workings. Rituals honor or mark certain events, such as solstices, equinoxes, moon phases, and rites of passage. Recording rituals may not seem as important as recording spells or divination, but it's part of building up a body of information about your green witch practice. There are two parts to recording your rituals: recording the planning stage and recording how the ritual went.

If you perform a spontaneous ritual (in other words, one from the heart with no planning beforehand), then there won't be a need to record the planning stage, obviously.

PLANNING

A record of the planning stage of a ritual is a valuable resource for future rituals. Start by writing about your goals, your ideas, the themes you want to touch on, and supplies or symbols you want to use. List the tools and materials you'll need. Summarize your intention in a statement that you can refer back to in the ritual and afterward. Next, write out the body of the ritual. Write new invocations or prayers, or use ones you have used previously and are comfortable with. You'll also want to plan the time and place you intend to perform the ritual. Note down whom you will perform the ritual with or for.

REFLECTION

Once you have performed the ritual, take the time to note down what you heard, how you felt, things that occurred to you while you conducted the ritual, and the like. Did you deviate from your written ritual? Did something happen that you hadn't planned for? How did the ritual affect you?

Do a brief reflection a few days later as well. Sometimes it takes your mind and spirit a while to process things. Note down any further insights.

RITUAL RECORD

1. PLANNING

Object/goal/purpose:

....

....

Key words:

....

....

Ideas:

....

....

Supplies/symbols to use:

....

....

Tools:

....

....

Central action:

....

....

2. WRITE OUT RITUAL

Statement of intent:

....
....
....
....
....

Invocations/ritual elements:

....
....
....
....
....

3. RECORD ACTION TAKEN

Date/time/place:

....

Additional desired info (weather, moon phase/sign, and so on):

....

Immediate report (how it felt, how it went, and so on):

....
....
....

ADD NOTES REGARDING CHANGES OR FUTURE IDEAS

_____
_____
_____
_____
_____
_____
_____

LEAVE SPACE FOR LATER REFLECTIONS AND FEEDBACK

_____
_____
_____
_____
_____
_____
_____
_____
_____
_____
_____
_____
_____

Here's an example of what a ritual record might look like.

RITUAL TO THANK GODS
FOR A WINDFALL

1. PLANNING

Object/goal/purpose:

To formally thank deity for the unexpected payment received

Key words:

gratitude, comfort, relief

Ideas:

Offering of fresh bread and local honey, freshly brewed mint tea

Mix dough, leave to rise before school drop-off; bake once back home; bread should be warm by ritual time

Pick mint for tea from garden after drop-off

Supplies/symbols to use:

Slice of freshly baked bread, small dish of local honey, mini teacup

Tools:

Offering bowl

Central action:

The presentation of bread and honey, with cup of tea, after statement of gratitude

2. WRITE OUT RITUAL

Statement of intent:

I thank you, Lord and Lady, for my great fortune in receiving this unexpected payment. Thank you for showing me that my work is valued and that I am appreciated so much more than I knew.

Invocations/ritual elements:

Usual quarter calls; usual circle cast; usual god/goddess invocations

Face western quarter for the statement to the gods, as that's the quarter associated with the work done. (Could do east, but west feels more appropriate right now.)

3. RECORD ACTION TAKEN

Date/time/place:

Thursday 3 October 2019, 10:15 a.m., family altar in the living room

Additional desired info (weather, moon phase/sign, and so on):

Clear, warm; waxing crescent

Immediate report (how it felt, how it went, and so on):

Nothing out of the ordinary

Felt very satisfying to offer back, especially using stuff I made/grew

ADD NOTES REGARDING CHANGES OR FUTURE IDEAS

Next time, pick herbs from garden, chop, and knead into bread; could make for a good Harvest offering

LEAVE SPACE FOR LATER REFLECTIONS AND FEEDBACK

Maybe do something like this quarterly, at solstices and equinoxes, as a general thanks for all the blessings received in that time frame?

Taking Notes

One aspect of recording information is noting down observations or interesting information as you read about and study various aspects of witchcraft and spirituality. These are study notes, things you want to remember, things that catch your attention, or things that are simply beautiful.

As in other places, you're going to have to decide where you're going to put the information you want to add to your grimoire. If it's about specific herbs, you could put it in your herbal reference section. If it's about historic or cultural practices, you might put it in a section marked *History*. Or perhaps you want all your study notes to go in their own section as you make them, with key information to be copied to specific locations later.

Always make note of where the information came from so you can reference it at a later date. The title of the book or article, the author, the URL if it is online or the book's ISBN are all valuable information pieces that can help you find the source again later. And trust me, you will not remember which source mentioned using lavender water for banishing fleas if someone calls you on the claim. Online sources are susceptible to vanishing, so if you feel the source is valuable enough, save it as a PDF.

EFFECTIVE NOTE-TAKING

If you're just reading something for interest's sake, then you might casually note down things that appeal to you or strike you in some way. If you're reading something to study it, however, you're more likely to remember key information if you intentionally take notes while reading. This kind of research is important to your development, because it underscores the intuitive knowledge you pick up from personal interaction with the world around you. Teaching yourself new things or reading analyses of topics you're interested in helps keep your brain active, and continually challenges your perceptions of the world around you.

It's important to take notes while you read for the following reasons:

- Noting down ideas and arguments while you read reinforces your memory of them. The act of physically recording them adds weight to the concept you're reading about and noting down.

- Taking notes as you read helps keep you focused. It keeps your attention active and stops the flow of words from becoming just a stream of information flowing past you.

Note-taking while reading is a different process from taking notes while listening to a lecture. Reading uses your eyes and attention, which you have to move and refocus in order to take notes. It's challenging. For a change of pace, see if the book you want to read is available as an audiobook, or an ebook that can be listened to via text-to-voice technology. Alternatively, see if the author has videos of their talks or documentaries on the subject.

Because you have to stop reading to take notes, it can be a slow process, and you risk running out of energy and patience during a study session. Use these tips to make the most of your reading time:

- Remember what your goal is. This will help you pick out the kind of information to take notes on. Why are you reading this book? What aspect of the topic are you currently focused on? What's your goal in this session?

- How do you intend to use the information you gain? Personal enrichment? To learn new techniques? The answers to these questions will further help focus your attention on the kind of note-taking to engage in.

- If you come across something cool or interesting that doesn't fit into the categories of what you're specifically reading for during this session, scribble it down in a margin or on a separate page, note the page number, and then let it go. Come back to it another time. This rewards your brain for going *Ooh, this is worth thinking about,* but it won't derail you from your goal for this particular study session.

CHAPTER 8

Journaling in Your Grimoire

ONE OF THE GRIMOIRE'S PURPOSES is to serve as a magical journal, a record of your practice and learning. It is a physical record of your work and spiritual journey. Journaling in general is an excellent practice that allows you to think about your current state, your dreams and goals, and your experiences, and how they relate to the world around you. Reflection and introspection are key concepts to using your grimoire to support your practice as a green witch, and journaling offers the opportunity for both.

Why Journaling Is Beneficial

Journaling gives you the opportunity to explore ideas and themes, uncover connections, and work out what issues are the most important to you in your practice, and it can also be an excellent stress reliever by helping you work out your fears or anxieties about something. Journaling can help you process events or emotions and help you become more aware of how your mind works. It provides insight into yourself.

You are able to gain this insight because when you write you engage the analytical and logic-based side of your brain. Once the logic side has something to occupy it, the other side of the brain—the side associated with creativity, free association, and emotion—is freer to express itself and is more easily accessed. Stream-of-consciousness writing can be very freeing, allowing you to act almost as a conduit for ideas and thoughts that you might not otherwise be able to consciously access.

> Writing things down signals to your brain that what it thinks and feels is important. This encourages it over time to be more willing to share with you. The more you journal, the easier it becomes to pin down and separate feelings.

Journaling can improve your mental and emotional health as well as your spiritual well-being. Journaling encourages mindfulness, a skill a green witch uses frequently. When you are mindful, you are paying attention to the small details all around you and using all your senses to absorb them. You are living just in that moment and listening to your subconscious, something that can help you gain valuable insight into why you do things you do. A journal allows you to cultivate a relationship with yourself, something that is important in a green witch's practice. Regular journaling also teaches self-discipline, another skill worth practicing.

Reasons for Journaling

Journaling serves a twofold purpose. First, it allows you to capture a moment and feeling. Second, it allows you to go back and consult that record sometime in the future. You may think you'll remember whatever you ought to journal about, but honestly, it can be difficult to do. Emotion and sensation are intense in the moment. That emotion is what makes you think you'll remember. But as the emotion fades, your detailed memory of it does, too, until all you remember is the fact that it had an impact. Identifying that impact is critical. Subtleties get lost as time passes.

Journaling also allows you to get to know yourself better. Like your grimoire that you work with as a whole, your journal very quickly begins to reflect your own energy, and in turn enhances the energy of the grimoire itself. Anything you write down carries energy and emotional impressions, and the aggregate of your records features not only data but the energy of your work as well. A journal in particular carries emotional energy and is an important element of your grimoire.

In addition, journaling is a way to release things: emotions that are overwhelming, anger, fears, and disturbing ideas that just won't leave you alone. Your journal can be a safe place to spill these out. Consider journaling these types of feelings and thoughts and then paper-clipping together the pages you've written on so that they don't become part of your review and reflection process. If you write specifically to release and exorcise something, rereading it can stir that emotion again and remind you of it. Even better, write your release journaling on a loose sheet of paper and then burn it.

Spiritual Journaling versus Mundane Journaling

When arranging your grimoire and deciding on its uses, one of the things to consider is whether the journal part of it will be exclusively spiritual or will encompass mundane issues as well.

A green witch doesn't usually separate spirituality from everyday life. We understand that the spiritual informs the mundane and that the two can rarely be completely divided from the other. Your spirituality will impact your life, just as your life will help shape your spirituality. That being said, you may want to keep a separate journal for everyday journaling to work out general issues, and a specific spiritual journal to think about issues and concepts you associate with your practice. They can both be part of your grimoire.

There is no right answer. Choose what is right for you. And as always, you can start one way and then switch to another if you discover that your initial plan doesn't serve your needs as well as you anticipated it would.

What to Journal

Journaling can be for reflecting on your day, musing about an abstract concept, recording insight, discussing an event and its impact, recording your experience wildcrafting or going on a nature walk—anything and everything.

A good way to begin is by taking a few minutes at the end of the day to write down what you are grateful for that happened during the day. You can challenge yourself to list five good things that happened that day, or note down anything that caught your attention.

Other things to journal about can include the following:

• Spiritual lessons you experienced or spiritual moments you had
• Good things you saw happen
• Your emotional response to the day's events
• Any time you felt inspired or close to Spirit
• Reflections on your spiritual goals

Once you're in the habit of journaling daily, your mind will start coming up with more things to write about.

So far, we've looked at journaling specifically associated with daily spiritual activity. There are other topics that belong in your spiritual journal as well:

- Dreams
- Meditations

Both dreams and meditations are a way of communicating with your subconscious, and are an opportunity for that subconscious to sort through ideas and impressions, processing your experiences. Journaling what you remember of them can be a valuable look into what your subconscious is currently processing. It's also a way to honor that process and the work your subconscious does, demonstrating that you value the work by taking the time to record. Writing down your impressions and images encountered in dreams and meditations also makes recalling them easier; the act itself of concentrating on remembering them seems to encourage more details to be recalled, making it easier over time.

Spiritual work stirs up the subconscious, which is often the first part of you to respond to that work. The subconscious is sensitive and uncontrolled; being in touch with it can be uncomfortable, but it is an important player in your spiritual expression. There's a lot that cannot be explained about spirituality. A lot of it is felt on a gut level, and this is where your subconscious comes in. So much spiritual work is done below the surface, and dreams and meditations allow you to glimpse part of that activity. Writing them down and thinking about the symbolism is as important in your spiritual journey as keeping track of your spells, divination, and rituals.

Should you handwrite or type your journal? Journaling is a tactile experience. A hands-on method is slower, allowing you to think as you go. However, if you honestly work better with digital journaling, do it. Use whatever app works for you, or make a private blog using whatever website or software you're comfortable with. You can print out your typed material and store it in a binder or keep it digital.

Training Yourself to Journal

Journaling is an important aspect of spiritual work. Ironically, it's something a lot of us resist doing. Whether it's because it feels like homework, or a waste of time because it has no immediate reward, lots of people drag their feet when it comes to this part of spiritual work. No one likes doing something just because it's good for them.

Retraining yourself to accept journaling as valid and important and incorporating it into working with your grimoire can be a daunting challenge. It requires discipline and a heavy dose of stubbornness. It's worth it, though. People who have practiced for years have discussed how grateful they are that their teachers made them journal right from the start, and some have lamented the fact that their early years were lost to time because they didn't journal the first steps of their path. Here are some tips for beginning (or think of them as refreshers if you've done this before):

- **Start with short sessions so you don't feel daunted.** Five minutes can be enough to jot down ideas or feelings in print form.

- **Set up a routine.** Our minds usually work well with routines because they decrease the time required to get into the right headspace for the next scheduled activity. So journal at roughly the same time in the same place every day. This can be while you're having your morning coffee or just before bed—whenever works best for you.

- **Always date your entries!** If you travel or are in a place that isn't your usual journaling location, note that down as well.

- **Write quickly and don't censor yourself.** Let the ideas go where they will. The entry doesn't have to make any kind of deep statement when you reread it. When you begin, you're training yourself to become familiar with the process, so don't listen to your internal editor or engage in negative self-talk. It doesn't have to be good, it just has to be done.

- **If you miss a day, don't beat yourself up.** But getting the rhythm going will create momentum, and every session will make the next one easier. The more days you miss, the harder it is to stick to.

- **Don't limit yourself to that journaling routine, however.** If you feel moved to journal something at another time, do it! Reward yourself for that urge. If you don't carry a journal around with you, use your smartphone notes app to tap things out, then recopy them to the journal later, or print them and paste them in.

Journaling Tips

Decide ahead of time what your focus for your journaling session will be. Are you writing to work out fears and anxieties about something specific, or to figure out what you're anxious about? Are you going to engage in stream-of-consciousness writing in order to try to capture ideas that you can't quite articulate yet? Having a goal will help focus your session and make your time more efficient. Here are some tips:

- Journal in a private, quiet place, and remember that your journal is for you alone.

- Treat your journaling time as self-care time. Create as comforting and peaceful an environment as possible.

- Try to make journaling a regular activity. If you journal only sporadically, you won't be able to read through your entries and discover connections or observations as easily. Regular journaling also supports self-discipline, and regular journaling activity eases the stress of doing it. Practice always makes things easier.

- If you're journaling to process something overwhelming or painful, don't feel that you have to write about the event or idea itself. Write around it instead, and be kind to yourself.

- If you are journaling to pinpoint a goal or to refine a focus, use statements such as *I feel* or *I think*. At the end of your session, summarize what you've figured out in a couple of sentences. This allows you to put a cap on your session and reaffirm to yourself that your time was well invested.

- Review what you wrote at various times; when depends on you. Journaling is a time to spill things out. Reviewing what you wrote about is equally valuable, because a bit of time and distance can help you view connections that you might not see in the moment.

Reflect On Your Journal Entries

Reflection should be an important part of your practice as a green witch. It is through reflection that we gain insight, which is part of how we grow and develop as spiritual beings. Reflecting on your journaling is a different process. You can look back at a specific time period, or look for a specific event if you're reminded of it. Reread entries, then write what you think of the ideas expressed in them from the point of view of an older, more experienced position. This enables you to actually observe your journey from the point of view of someone else. Here are some tips for reflection on your journal:

- Around once a month, reread the previous month's worth of entries to get a sense of how that month went. Write an entry reflecting on the month's journey.

- Reread your entries regularly (seasonally, monthly, whatever works for you; do it more than annually, though, because reviewing an entire year of activity is a heavy undertaking).

- To reflect on your spiritual development, choose a longer period of time between writing and reviewing. It's harder to see small changes within shorter periods of time.

Magical journaling is partly for recording your magical activity (see the previous chapter, which discusses recording rituals, spellwork, and so forth), but also allowing you time and space to think about spiritual concepts. Journaling is a dialogue with yourself and offers you the chance to think aloud, as it were. Spiritual concepts and connections can take some time to comprehend, and our relationship to them grows and shifts and changes over time. Journaling allows you to explore those changes and the evolution of your opinion and response to various ideas.

Journaling Prompts

If you're having trouble thinking of something to write about, try some of these prompts:

- **Color.** Pick a color. Visualize things in that color. Visualize the color drifting in the air in front of you; visualize breathing it in. How does it make you feel? If you have trouble visualizing, go to the hardware store and gather paint chips in a few different colors and cut them into separate pieces. Look at the color on one chip and be open to receiving ideas and feelings that it elicits in you.

- **Sound.** Find a recording of a particular sound, such as a bell or a singing bowl, and listen to it. Notice the feelings and impressions that arise in you in response to the sound. Write them down as they come.

- **Daily responses.** Write how you responded to things that caught your attention or that stood out in some way today.

- **Weekly review.** Write an overall view of the week that has just passed.

- **Monthly review.** Write an overall view of month that has just passed, and set intentions/goals for the upcoming month.

- **Seasonal concerns.** Sense how energy shifts as the seasons move through their cycle. What energies and changes do you sense? What do the changes make you think of or feel? Be open to noticing how the energies shift minutely over time, not all at once like when a big switch is thrown.

- **Special days/anniversaries.** How does remembering these events make you feel?

- **Moon phases.** How do your personal energies shift in response to the moon going through its cycle?

- **Weather.** How do different kinds of weather make you feel?

CHAPTER 9

Honoring Your Grimoire

AS A GREEN WITCH, you walk your spiritual path because to do anything else wouldn't make sense. You resonate with the cyclic rhythms of nature, and you know that you and nature are inextricably intertwined. Your grimoire reflects your ideals, values, and work within those natural cycles. This chapter explores how to consciously take the morals and ethics encoded in it and apply them in the mundane world. That may seem a contradiction; after all, green witches live their spirituality. However, there is often a divide where you unconsciously think about your spiritual life and your day-to-day life as a pair of paths that have an effect on each other, but are not fundamentally the same.

Should they be? It's an excellent question. (Quick, go mull it over in your magical journal to capture your initial ideas before you read any further!) It can be argued that a practitioner ought to infuse their daily life with magic and consider every act a spiritual one, but that also suggests that we have to live every second of our lives with active awareness. That would be overwhelming. How can you bring your spiritual and mundane lives into a closer, overlapping relationship?

The answer is by making sure your ethical system is the same within both. That may sound obvious, and you probably assume that the same ethical system is at work in both spheres. However, it's worth thinking it through to see if that's actually the case. This chapter will help you do that.

Your Grimoire As a Record of Your Values

Constant revisiting of your ethics is important. You are, after all, a constantly evolving person; neither you nor your ethical system are made of stone. (And even if you were, time and the elements wear away at stone to reshape it.) Every experience you have will contribute to your moral and ethical outlook. An ethical system should be consistent, but that doesn't mean it shouldn't grow and evolve.

Your grimoire is not only a record of practical information within a spiritual context. It is also an evolving record of how your spiritual practice impacts your everyday life. Your grimoire becomes a record of your ethical system and how you implement it, how you react to the world, and how you observe that it affects you.

The act of reflecting and writing things down makes you more aware of how you process these things. It makes you more likely to examine your behavior in a contemplative way as you encounter situations in your daily life that require you to make decisions. Increased awareness leads to a continual refining of your ethics and how you implement them in your day-to-day life. In this way, your grimoire becomes an important partici- pant in your work to bring your spiritual ethics into your mun- dane life.

Your grimoire and its contents become part of a cycle wherein you record your activity, analyze that activity, apply your con- clusions or ideas to refine your ethical approach, and so on. Reviewing your records offers you a way to search for themes and concepts that resonate with you, and to pick out values that are reflected in your choices and responses.

A lot of reflection on ethics is important in order to be as true to yourself as possible and stay in touch with the flow of your spiritual life. It's easy to get stuck in a rut, doing the same thing repeatedly, but habit is no substitute for ongoing reevalu- ation of who you are and how well you are living your truth. Your grimoire plays a critical role in this ongoing reflection, providing a place to record, reflect, and work out tricky issues. It's not an easy task, but it's an important one. Taking shortcuts in your spirituality is pointless. It does nothing to support your spiritual growth and work to become the best version of yourself that you can be at any given moment.

Morals and Ethics: A Quick Look

The terms *morals* and *ethics* are often used interchangeably, but there is a difference in how they are applied. Morals are the values you hold that help you define right from wrong. The concept of morals is often considered subjective. The idea of morality is usually associated with correct behavior at large. The word's root comes from the Latin *moralis*, meaning "a custom."

Ethics are a specific application, such as the discussion of the objective morals of something like corporal punishment or eugenics. The concept of ethics is sometimes considered more objective and is applied to what constitutes correct behavior in a specific group, or in terms of objective fairness or rightness. Words like *ought* or *should* are often used when considering ethical issues. Ethics are how you apply your morals; hence the use of the term *ethical system*. The word's root comes from the Greek *ēthikos*, which is also the root of *etiquette*.

Both morals and ethics rest on the values you consider important to uphold. A value is a quality or concept that you define as worthy, such as honesty, kindness, or justice.

Using these definitions, an act you consider unethical would be something that contravenes your personal morals.

A cultural group has shared ethical values that define right and wrong. Ethical systems are not absolute, however. Every individual within that system has a slightly different set of personal ethics, because each individual's point of view differs from the next person's. The cultural ethical system broadly defines right and wrong; the personal ethical system further refines that at the personal level. A choice you make is very rarely 100 percent right or wrong. There are usually better choices and poorer choices, but what may constitute a better choice for you may not be the better choice for someone else.

Religious groups also have ethical systems, which often overlap with cultural ethics. Civic morals may be based in religious morality but function separate from it. (For example, religions may teach that murder is ethically wrong and warn of punishment to come in the afterlife; civic ethical systems define it as illegal and mete out civic punishment.)

MORAL REASONING AND ETHICAL COMPLEXITY

American psychologist Lawrence Kohlberg, who studied the field of moral development and moral judgment, created a six-step description of how moral reasoning becomes increasingly complex when ethical practices are addressed. His student Carol Gilligan added an extra observation about the function of empathy in the reasoning operation that adds an important dimension to the process, especially within a spiritual context. A green witch tries to function with the wellness of everything in mind, including the energy of the environment around them.

Similar to Maslow's hierarchy of needs, Kohlberg's stages increase in sophistication, with each step dependent on completing or fulfilling the one before it. The sophistication of steps also reflects the more complex situations a developing individual finds themselves in; for example, a child usually operates within a family unit, then a larger educational unit, then a larger community. The more people involved, the more complex the ethical reasoning becomes, and the more people have to rely on a social contract to function within a society.

LAWRENCE KOHLBERG'S SIX STAGES OF MORAL REASONING (Plus Carol Gilligan's Orthogonal Axis of Ethical Care)

1. *"Stage 1: Punishment-avoidance and obedience—Individuals make moral decisions on the basis of what is best for themselves, without regard for the needs or feelings of others. They obey rules only if established by more powerful individuals; they disobey when they can do so without getting caught.*

2. *"Stage 2: Exchange of favors—Individuals begin to recognize that others also have needs. They may attempt to satisfy the needs of others if their own needs are also met in the process. They continue to define right and wrong primarily in terms of consequences to themselves.*

3. *"Stage 3: Good boy/good girl—Individuals make moral decisions on the basis of what actions will please others, especially authority figures. They are concerned about maintaining interpersonal relationships through sharing, trust, and loyalty. They now consider someone's intentions in determining innocence or guilt.*

4. **"Stage 4: Law and order**—*Individuals look to society as a whole for guidelines concerning what is right or wrong. They perceive rules to be inflexible and believe that it is their "duty" to obey them.*

5. **"Stage 5: Social contract**—*Individuals recognize that rules represent an agreement among many people about appropriate behavior. They recognize that rules are flexible and can be changed if they no longer meet society's needs.*

6. **"Stage 6: Universal ethical principle**—*Individuals adhere to a small number of abstract, universal principles that transcend specific, concrete rules. They answer to an inner conscience and may break rules that violate their own ethical principles.*

7. **"Orthogonal axis: Ethics of care**—*An obligation of care rests on the understanding of relationships as a response to another in terms of their special needs. Focuses on the moral value of being empathetic toward those dearly beloved persons with whom we have special and valuable relationships, and the moral importance of responding to such persons as unique individuals with characteristics that require custom-crafted responses to them that we do not normally extend to others."*

That's as complicated as we're going to get right now on the subject. I've included Kohlberg's six stages to provide food for thought as you begin to explore your own concept of ethics, morals, and values and how they function within your spiritual sphere and your mundane (or nonmagical) sphere.

Read Kohlberg's moral stages. Journal a response to each stage. How do they make you feel? Do they raise any questions? How does Carol Gilligan's orthogonal axis modify or enhance your perception of each of the stages?

Spiritual Ethics versus Mundane Ethics

If you think back to the earlier paragraph about the response to murder in a religious versus civic context, you can see that civic, or mundane, ethics can parallel religious ethics, but they are not identical. And one does not necessarily replace the other.

For this reason, it's important to sit down and really think about your spiritual ethics and your mundane ethics and see how they differ. Remember, differing isn't necessarily bad or good; it's simply a fact. Your values are what ascribe importance to your morals.

Situational ethics is a term that describes how your personal ethical system may flex or be fluid according to the circumstances. To use the example of murder, in general we can agree that killing is wrong. What happens to the value of respecting human life when there is a single person holding a dozen others hostage with the intent to kill them all to make a point? Ideally, the individual would be neutralized without death, but what if the case is extreme and it is one human life against twelve others?

There is no right answer. There are, as mentioned earlier, degrees of right and wrong; sometimes one decision is less bad than another but still can't be classified as good. And most important of all, as the one in charge of your spirituality, you bear responsibility for your choices and actions. Defining your ethical system can be very challenging, and uncomfortable to boot. Be gentle to yourself, and remember that you don't have to do it all at once. It's an ongoing process.

EXERCISE: SPIRITUAL ETHICS

The point of this exercise is to try to define your spiritual eth-ics. Don't do this exercise and the following exercise back-to-back on the same day. Give yourself time between them (preferably at least a day), and don't refer back to your notes on spiritual ethics until after you have completed the mundane version of the exercise.

WHAT YOU NEED
- White candle in candleholder
- Matches or lighter
- Incense and censer (if desired)
- Grimoire
- Pen

WHAT TO DO
1. Set up your work area. Light the candle with a brief prayer, if you like, asking the Divine, the universe, or Nature to help you as you explore this subject. Light incense if you

so desire; use a light scent associated with spirituality, such as lotus, jasmine, or sandalwood.

2. Take a moment to center and ground. Do a bit of breathing meditation if you like.

3. Ask yourself:

What spiritual values do I consider important?
How do I embody or honor each of these values while walking my spiritual path?
What aspects of my spiritual path reflect each of these values?

4. Write down your answers in your grimoire.

EXERCISE: MUNDANE ETHICS

The point of this exercise is to try to define your ethical system in a mundane, or day-to-day, context.

WHAT YOU NEED

- White candle in candleholder
- Matches or lighter
- Incense and censer (if desired)
- Grimoire
- Pen

WHAT TO DO

1. Set up your work area. Light the candle with a brief prayer, if you like, asking the Divine, the universe, or Nature to help you as you explore this subject. Light incense if you so desire; use an earthy scent that helps with grounding, such as patchouli or pine.

2. Take a moment to center and ground. Do a bit of breathing meditation if you like.

3. Ask yourself:

   What daily values do I consider important?
   How do I embody or honor each of these values in my daily life?
   What aspects of my life reflect each of these values?

4. Write down your answers in your grimoire.

5. A day or more after you have completed both exercises, sit down with your grimoire and compare the two lists. Where do they overlap? Where do they differ? Do the similarities bother you? Do the differences bother you, or do they make sense? Journal your ideas.

ETHICAL QUESTIONS TO PONDER

Sometimes just thinking about a subject can be difficult. Here are some ethical questions to ask yourself to help pin down the values you hold and contexts for them.

SPIRITUAL QUESTIONS

- Would you charge for helping someone out with magical-associated problems?
- If someone offered to pay you for help, would you accept their money?
- Would you ask them to cover the cost of supplies, but not accept money for the actual energy work?
- Would you haggle about the price of a tool that you intend to use in your spiritual practice?
- Would you negotiate the price of something associated with your spiritual practice that is being handcrafted for you?
- Would you ask a specific payment for performing a rite of passage ceremony?
- Would you ask for a freewill offering for performing a rite of passage ceremony?
- Would you refuse payment for a rite of passage ceremony if it was offered?

MUNDANE QUESTIONS

- Do you work at a company or with an organization that has a defined code of conduct? Are you comfortable within it?

- Have you ever had to report something that contravened the code of conduct?
- Have you ever observed a contravention of the code of conduct and not reported it? If so, why?
- Who would you go to if you observed an ethical issue in the workplace?
- How does your company's code of ethics align with or differ from your personal code of ethics?
- Do you feel that your coworkers' values align with your own?
- In your circle of friends, do you feel that your values align with theirs?
- What differences in your ethical systems can you accept? What differences can you not reconcile?
- When there are differences too great to reconcile in a relationship of any kind, what do you do? How do you handle the dissonance?

GENERAL QUESTIONS

- Is empathy a spiritual value, or a mundane one?
- Is justice a spiritual value, or a mundane one?
- How does blame function as part of ethics?
- What is the function of responsibility in the practice of ethics?

Integrating the Spiritual and Mundane Ethical Systems

—◦◦◦◦—

You may have intuited by now that it's important for your mundane ethical system and your spiritual ethical system to stay in relative balance with each other in order to minimize dissonance and stress. If they are wildly different, then you're setting yourself up for fighting yourself. If you are miserable in your job, take a look at the corporate ethical practices and compare them to your own, both mundane and spiritual. It's entirely likely that they vary enough to make you uncomfortable.

Once you've had a good long think about the ethical systems in the two different areas of your life, the next question to ask yourself is how to integrate the two systems. More specifically, how can you bring your spiritual ethical system into your mundane life?

Ask yourself:

- How does my spiritual life influence my mundane life?
- How does my mundane life impact my spiritual goals?
- How does my life in general reflect my spirituality?

You can also design a set of affirmations underscoring/supporting your ethical beliefs to use in various areas of your life. Using these will help carry your energy throughout all areas of your life and help even out/make more sympathetic the energy between different aspects of your life.

OUTLINING YOUR SPIRITUAL GOALS

Outlining your spiritual goals in your grimoire is another way to create dialogue with yourself about your ethics. First, look at the list of spiritual values that you made in the earlier exercise.

- What would you like to change?
- What do you want to support?
- What do you want to rework?
- How do you integrate the spiritual goals into your day-to-day life?
- How can you live your mundane life in a way that supports your spiritual goals?

ETHICS WRAP-UP

There are no universal answers to these questions nor answers that are absolutely right or wrong. A set of step-by-step instructions in a handy book does not, and cannot, exist. The only person who can answer these questions about your morals, ethics, and values is yourself, and only you can design a plan to balance your mundane and spiritual goals so that they support and reinforce one another.

It's not an easy thing to do, and it will be an ongoing process. Like with so many other spiritual undertakings, your process will change as you yourself change; your needs are fluid, and your desire for expression will alter as time passes. Honor the fact that your needs will differ from time to time, and treat yourself with respect.

Honoring Your Personal Body of Wisdom

With your grimoire and its contents reflecting your accrual of wisdom and knowledge, both about the natural world and the world of your own spirit, you can walk through the world with new awareness, insight, and inspiration. Honor your grimoire and its collection of your spiritual work and reflection by walking the talk, so to speak. What does that mean?

WALKING THE TALK

Walking the talk doesn't mean being obvious and theatrical about your spirituality so that everyone knows. It means behaving and acting true to your ethics, and being the example to show others that working to improve oneself and the world around them is a valuable undertaking.

It also means bringing your spiritual ethics into your daily life. Through the previous exercises and thought work, you've seen that it's important for your mundane ethical system and your spiritual ethical system to stay in relative balance with each other in order to minimize dissonance and stress in your life. Review the exercises and questions posed earlier in this chapter on a regular basis—perhaps annually—to make sure you're staying true to your current values and ethical system.

Remember, they aren't absolute and eternal. Your experiences will have an effect on your morals, and you deserve the opportunity to stay true to your most current set in order to be the most authentic version of you that you can be.

What if you review your records and journaling to discover that you don't like where your ethical system is headed? Then it's time to set up a new series of affirmations written to help you focus on the values you actively want your behavior to reflect.

Witnessing

Honoring your grimoire in the world also means witnessing what is happening to the natural world. Witnessing doesn't just mean observing. It means being present and aware so that someone will remember the events, someone who respects and loves the natural world. To witness something happening is to honor it. It's recognizing and affirming that it exists and that it is happening. To bear witness to something is to confirm its truth. Sometimes it's as simple as recognizing what is happening. There doesn't have to be a big production; simply seeing it for what it is and bearing witness to it can be enough. Acknowledging it with dignity to the land is meaningful as well. You can write a ritual to do this or speak from the heart.

Witnessing can be difficult to do, because it means you have to take in the information objectively. It's easy enough to witness a sunrise. It's a challenge to be objective in the face of the death and destruction going on in the world around you.

Witnessing is an important act for a green witch. A green witch works with natural cycles and recognizes that every stage of a cycle is as important as the others. At no time is a part of the cycle weaker or unimportant; every part helps balance the whole. Witnessing every stage is important, giving honor where it is due. Something that your grimoire can do is help you work with and witness the more difficult part of the cycle, the part that people shy away from: death.

HONORING DEATH AS PART OF THE NATURAL CYCLE

Analyzing how you feel about the death portion of the natural cycle is tricky. There's a lot of emotion wound up in it, and it can be hard to separate the concept from your personal experience with it via the death of a pet, a family member, or one of your heroes.

Personal experience and the associated emotion are absolutely part of your relationship with death. We internalize and form a dialogue with a concept through personal experience. But as a green witch, you have to look beyond your personal experience to observe the world at large.

Marking each stage of a cycle is important; it helps us affirm the cycle and reassure ourselves that things are always moving, always in a state of change. This can be reassuring, but it can also be a cause of anxiety; like the Wheel of Fortune card from the tarot deck's Major Arcana cards symbolizes, good things or periods of expansion don't last forever. Conversely, difficult times will pass, which may be a comfort.

Human beings are very good at noticing things that are encouraging or that bring them joy. They are also very good at avoiding dealing with things that scare or stress them. (This avoidance can in turn cause more stress, something else we are very good at doing.) It's destructive to ignore the part of the life cycle that deals with diminishment and death.

Your records and journal section of your grimoire are important partners in your witnessing of the darker half of the cycle of expansion and diminishment. As you observe the seasons shifting and the other ways that the cycle of growth, withering, and rebirth demonstrates itself, your records of your observations will begin to form a deeper understanding of that portion of the cycle. Marking each stage of the cycle is important for a green witch, and honoring death within that cycle is something that needs to be done more often.

Death—of a life form, an era, a smaller cycle within the cycle at large—is very important. It allows a release of energy so that the cycle may continue properly. It also allows you to release a personal connection to a situation or whatever the subject and/or object may be. This is why Samhain and other harvest rituals can be important; besides giving us the chance to express gratitude or commemorate ancestors, they allow us to take stock of what has come to an end in our lives, to release things that no longer benefit us, and to acknowledge that death is a natural part of every cycle. Recognizing the place and purpose death serves in the cycle offers insight.

Earlier this chapter described the act of witnessing as a form of honoring energy and the associated action being undertaken or occurring. For a green witch, honoring death is important, and bearing witness to it (in whatever form) honors the energy and the release or transformation involved.

This is part of serving as clergy for the natural world. This is a step beyond practicing nature-based spirituality, which focuses on you and your relationship with the natural world. Serving as clergy for nature itself can be compared to being a doula at a birth: You are there to support, comfort, and bear witness during times of change.

WRITE A RITUAL TO HONOR DEATH

Meditate on the concept of death (the step prior to birth) as part of the natural cycle, a release of energy to further the cycle and advance the rhythm of nature. Note down ideas and images as they occur to you—gratitude, solemnity, joy, change, transformation, or whatever comes to mind. There are no incorrect responses.

Create a ritual that expresses honor for death. It may be gestures, dance, spoken word, written verse, or art; ritual does not always need to be formal words at an altar. In this ritual, seek to express your innermost sense of death and what it means within the natural cycle, and to you as part of that cycle.

A ritual like this can be created anew and performed at the end of something, even thoughts or beliefs. Ritually releasing these can allow you to process and absorb the impact of this point in the cycle.

These are suggestions alone, and left as such deliberately to encourage you to reach out to communicate with the earth's energy and to intuitively respond.

Keep notes on your experiences; journal them, record any rituals you do (either planned or spontaneous), and meditate about them. Death and endings are a difficult part of the life cycle to comprehend, especially on a grand scale. Allow yourself the room to experience your emotions, and honor them.

THE PAIN OF THE LAND

Witnessing natural disasters, even secondhand via the news, is traumatic and heartrending. We are the earth; we are part of its body, just as all living things are. To watch nature be battered by droughts, fires, and earthquakes affects us. The web of energy that connects all natural things on earth means these things impact us, too, whether we are there in person or not. Sympathy and empathy with those creatures affected by these disasters means we often feel called to work magic on their behalf.

RESPONDING MAGICALLY TO
NATURAL DISASTERS

Fires, floods, earthquakes, droughts, climate change, and uncertain or shifting growing seasons impact our world, and if all you are in a position to do is donate funds and/or do energy work, then do that. No act is too small. Another way to engage is to acknowledge the disaster, to mourn or express anger in a ritual setting, if you feel you need to. As a steward of the land and one who communicates with the spirit of Nature, the need to help during crises can be almost painful.

Part of acting in the spirit of your grimoire is engaging with the needs of the land. Responding magically to a disaster by communicating with the land helps both you and the earth itself. You don't need to be present at the site of a natural disaster; you can communicate with the energy of the earth to intuit what it might need.

Meditate on the natural disaster you are working to help. Note down images or emotions, and use your intuition to divine what the affected area could benefit from. You're not trying to solve the disaster or reverse it. Ask yourself what the land needs to cope with the aftermath and recovery. The answer doesn't have to be rain if it's a drought or wildfire; think beyond the physical solution and ask yourself what sort of energy the land could use. Healing energy is another obvious answer. Open your heart and mind to different answers, and write them down in your grimoire.

Raising energy can be done physically—dancing, singing, or humming, for example—emotionally, or by act of will.

Remember, center and ground yourself before engaging in any of these; it is very easy to draw on your own finite energy to send toward a goal and then realize that you haven't enough left for yourself to operate safely. It can take days to recover from a miscalculation like this. These are suggestions alone, and left as such deliberately to encourage you to reach out to communicate with the earth's energy and intuitively respond.

Write down your ritual when it is complete. If it was brainstormed and performed spontaneously, write down the experience and as much information as you can.

REFLECT ON BEING CLERGY FOR NATURE

In the journal section of your grimoire, brainstorm ideas and concepts you associate with serving as clergy for Nature. What do you think are Nature's needs? How can you meet them? How can you express your spiritual goals and ethics while serving as a priestess or priest for Nature itself?

This exercise may take time. You may think of things as the seasons change or as momentous natural events take place. Note them down in this section reserved for reflection.

As in other cases, your opinions and feelings on the matter will change over time. Note the date down at the beginning of a new thought or idea so that you can trace your evolution.

Representing Your Grimoire in the Everyday World

Don't dismiss the value of your behavior and outlook being an example to your community and social circles. Carrying the spirit of your grimoire out into the world means that you recognize and respect the natural world and are dedicated to serving it. Follow your intuition, be open to impressions and the movement of energy, and serve the earth as best you can.

One of the ways to do this is recognizing the sacred in the mundane. The world you walk through is blessed; there is no separation between the everyday world and the world of spirituality. The divine spirit of Nature manifests in the people you pass on the street, the breeze that moves the air around you, and the clouds that pass in front of the sun. Every step you take, you take in sacred space.

The choices you make and your behavior serve as an example to those around you. Picking up extra litter after eating outside for lunch or carrying a reusable travel mug reminds your colleagues that small gestures are easy to implement. Collecting discarded takeout wrappers or coffee cups isn't going to change the world, but it demonstrates that someone cares. Putting a human face on respecting the environment is sometimes all it takes to inspire someone else to make a small tweak in their own lives. The ocean is made up of millions of drops of water, after all. And encouraging respect is a noble goal. If there were more respect in general—for people, ideas, nature—the world would be a healthier, happier place.

Finally, outreach can be inspiring as well. Talk to your HR department about its charities or fundraising activities, and suggest causes that you have vetted ahead of time that run their foundations with business practices that respect their workers and the environment. Invite friends over for a postcard-writing campaign for a cause close to your heart, and ask them about their causes too. Talk to your children's teachers and ask if there's a way to incorporate awareness into their curriculum; perhaps offer to run an activity for them that raises awareness about local shelters, or municipal council efforts to overhaul a park or plant trees. Demonstrating engagement can be very inspiring. Setting an example for the people in your personal sphere can have further repercussions than you might know.

CHAPTER 10

Personal Development Within the Green Witch Path

GREEN WITCHCRAFT IS ABOUT PERSONAL DEVELOPMENT in the context of natural energy communication and work. This is not necessarily always happy energy that you work with, as you have no doubt already discovered. As green witches, we don't have to like or dislike something; the only requirement is that we respect it.

Green witchcraft is also about transformation. We transform the supplies we use in spellcrafting to help us reach a goal; we witness the seasons shifting from one to another; and most important of all, we witness our own transformation day by day into a better version of ourselves. That requires more than witnessing, however. We need to actively pursue that transformation. This chapter explores personal development in the context of your grimoire and work done in partnership with it.

Developing As a Green Witch

You are an ongoing project. There will never be a time when you are considered complete and finished; as you grow and learn, there will always be something more you can do and ways you can refine and improve yourself. Your grimoire is your partner through this process. Think of it as a reflection of your true spirit, a place where you can sift through ideas to inspire you and generate new ways of thinking about information. In order to make this work, however, you have to do the work of collecting and creating your grimoire's contents.

On one hand, a grimoire is a collection of rituals, spells, recipes, and the like, as discussed in Chapter 1. On the other, it needs to be a place where you record personal musings, experiences, meditations, results of spells, and so forth, crafting a reflection of your spiritual journey and understanding of the natural world around you. These two halves of your grimoire work together to be a foundation and valuable resource in deepening your practice of green witchcraft.

Don't dismiss small changes. Often, you may not even notice you're evolving until one day you look at an old journal entry or ritual you created and realize that you'd never react that way now or approach a ritual that way. Every encounter you have and every bit of information you come across can affect you in ways you can't foresee. This is one of the reasons that journaling is so important. Being able to look back and find where something began is critical. Even more valuable is being able to read through your records and trace the evolution.

Finding Balance

One of the most difficult things to do is lead a balanced life. It's a constant dance and adjustment, because there is no such thing as permanent balance. There can't be, because energy is in constant motion. You are fluid, not static. You are constantly shifting in response to the energy moving around you, as well as within you. Think of a ball filled with water. As it rolls, the water inside shifts and alters the trajectory of the ball to some extent.

JOURNAL PROMPT: BALANCE

Take out your grimoire, go to your journal section, and ponder the idea of balance. How do you define balance? When do you feel balanced? How can you identify when you are out of balance?

Figuring out balance is tricky. Your grimoire is of great use here. Review your magical journal and your spell and ritual records. What comes up again and again as an obstacle or challenge for you? What are the periods where everything seems to be in sync in your life? What patterns can you discern? Is there a common theme you work to achieve?

Sometimes the energy around you gets wonky. Your environment is affected by the people moving through it, the natural objects and greenery in it, and the natural flow of energy in and through. Energy can pool in areas that don't see a lot of movement or interaction, and it can go stagnant. You can work to improve the energy of an area, or neutralize negative energy that has gathered, all for the general good. Remember to consult the area itself, however, by opening yourself to impressions and responses and asking what it wants done and how it wants things to be handled. Don't make a decision and impose it without consulting first.

The world at large is a different matter. Again, as I pointed out in the previous chapter, you can't fix something that enormous alone. Work at the level you are able and support others however you can.

Connecting to Your Local Environment

Local plants, rocks, and animals may not seem as exciting as those spoken of in traditional practice, handed down in folklore, but these things are the building blocks that form the foundation of your local environment's energy. There is nothing that carries more power than the natural environment around you. Consider what connection you have to a rare wood harvested on another continent, processed, packaged, and shipped to your location, and compare that to a sample of wood taken from half a mile away from where you live.

Purists may argue that the sample of rare wood contains within it an energy that is strong enough for people to make personal connections with and to rise above the difference in geographic origin. To be perfectly honest, there are few foreign things for which you cannot find a local equivalent or analog. Pine or cedar can be substituted for sandalwood, for example. If you feel you absolutely must have a certain thing, try to source it from your own continent, at least. Copal can be substituted for frankincense in a lot of situations, for instance. Yes, the resonance and energy will be different, but so is your environment in which you're working magic. Doesn't it make sense to use something more in tune with your environment rather than something foreign?

To facilitate this experience, you'll need to study facts and history about your geographic location. You may be quite surprised at some of the things you find out. We tend to research faraway places because they seem exotic and unusual to us, but there is plenty to learn about right outside our doors. Discover the magic of your own home base. Research these things and note them in your grimoire:

- **Geography:** Read up on your local geography and the types of environments it hosts. Visit as many as you can to be physically present and get a sense of the energy each holds. Visit one location in all four seasons, observing the physical and energy shifts. What changes? What stays the same?

Record your observations in your journal. Reflect on your geographic location and its environments. Is there an area that is sacred to a community or culture, or to you personally? (Remember to respect restrictions.)

- **Fauna:** Read about the animals native to your area. Birds and bugs are the most likely to be observed in person if you go out and look for them; look up their energies and meanings only after you've meditated on them to discover what meaning they hold for you without being influenced by whatever body of knowledge already exists.

- **Stones:** Look up what geological information you can about your area. You can work with stones and crystals from shops that come from other places, of course, but stones from your immediate geographic area form part of the energy you're already connected to. If you can't find correspondences for the types of rock in your area, meditate and do the energy-sensing exercise in Chapter 6 with samples of rock and list your own correspondences. You can do powerful magic using materials native to your location.

Connecting to Your Supplies and Materials

Your grimoire can serve as a guide for deepening your connection to the energy of your supplies and materials that you use in your practice. In some of my other books, I've written about enhancing the innate energies of natural supplies by empowering them or drawing forth the ingredient's energy in a specific way to best resonate with and support your goal. Here, I'm going to look at how honoring your supplies can strengthen your general connection to the natural world and your overall practice.

SOURCE YOUR SUPPLIES RESPONSIBLY

Know where your supplies and materials come from, as best you can. The previous section mentioned using supplies sourced locally because of their sympathetic resonance with your geographic location. Be aware of the environmental impact of the industry associated with the supplies you consume as well. Look into the company selling the product. Are its trade ethics transparent? Does it fairly pay its workers? If the company acquires its ingredients from elsewhere, can you track the chain further and ask the same questions all the way along? Can the company guarantee the authenticity of the product it's selling, or is it a case of cassia commonly being sold as Ceylon cinnamon? (They're both varieties of cinnamon, and they have a similar flavor profile, but the complexities of taste beyond that are different.) That's a cooking example, but the analogy is sound.

Learning to sense energy and interpret it is one of the most valuable skills you have as a green witch. If a dried and crumbled sample of a plant feels very different from another sample you read at an earlier time, try to figure out why. (You can look back to the extensive notes in your grimoire that you took the first time you worked with the plant and compare them to this time.) Mistaken plant identification? Heavily influenced by energies where it was grown? Or is it another plant entirely, either by error or in a deliberate attempt on the part of the supplier to cut corners or otherwise save money?

Stones and crystals can easily fall victim to this kind of shady business practice. Is that an actual rose quartz, or is it artificially dyed quartz? Is that a citrine, or is it a heat-treated amethyst that has turned yellow or pale brown? (Partial heat-treating results in what scientists call an *ametrine*, and it would have its own energy, not that of amethyst or citrine. Experiment!) The mining practices may negatively impact the environment around the mine.

It can be frustrating, especially when all you want to do is work with natural energies. But to properly honor your grimoire and be honest in your practice, these are all issues that you should think about.

HONOR YOUR SUPPLIES

Your supplies are part of the earth, just as you are, and as such they deserve respect. Think of them as partners in your work. Thank them when you use them, and appreciate the fact that they bring energy and potential. This quotation from Robin Wall Kimmerer in her book titled *Braiding Sweetgrass* sums up this idea:

> *Know the ways of the ones who take care of you, so that*
> *you may take care of them.*
> *Introduce yourself. Be accountable as the one who*
> *comes asking for life.*
> *Ask permission before taking. Abide by the answer.*
> *Never take the first. Never take the last. Take only what*
> *you need.*
> *Take only that which is given.*

Never take more than half. Leave some for others. Harvest in a way that minimizes harm.
Use it respectfully. Never waste what you have taken. Share.
Give thanks for what you have been given.
Give a gift, in reciprocity for what you have taken.
Sustain the ones who sustain you and the earth will last forever.

A way to honor your supplies includes being cognizant of their origins and their cultural associations. Smudging with white sage, for example, originated as a sacred ceremony with North American indigenous tribes and has been co-opted by wellness trends. Not only has this put a strain on the supply of ceremonial sage, but the appropriation is disrespectful to the indigenous peoples who had their cultural practices made illegal. Use alternate herbs harvested in a sustainable way, and use the term *smoke cleansing* instead of *smudging*.

Be intentional with your spiritual practice. Gather as much information about the origin of your supplies and the practices used to harvest and process them as you can in order to practice with awareness.

Remind yourself of this regularly by adding a line of gratitude and acknowledgment when you are using materials harvested or gathered by you or anyone else:

Thank you, [herbs/stones/materials], for sharing your energy with me.
I acknowledge your connection to Nature and honor it.

Healing

Healing is one of the green witch's purviews, and likely something that you want to work on often, whether it be for yourself or various places or issues nature is facing. Don't think of healing as "fixing." Think of it as restoring things to a neutral position, or to the optimal state for that specific point of time. Use phrases or imagery along with words like "with the goal of achieving the ultimate positive state" to think of healing as a moving process, not a one-shot cure. Think of it as facilitating or easing the flow of constructive, supportive energy along the channels it needs to travel.

JOURNAL PROMPT: HEALING

In your grimoire write about the idea of healing. How do you define healing? What are the steps involved in healing? How do you identify something as being in need of healing? How would you judge that need to have been met and the object healed?

Like redressing imbalance, healing entails altering the balance of helpful and unhelpful energy. (I don't use the words *positive* and *negative* energy, because there are energies qualified as positive that can be unhelpful for specific goals.) A large part of healing yourself is releasing what doesn't serve you well. This can be outdated things, or energy that might be positive but that doesn't help you where you are at present, and might even be pulling you off course. It may feel odd to consider releasing positive energy, but just think about it. If you need a specific vitamin to beef up your health in a particular way, you eat a specific kind of food. Other foods are good, but they don't necessarily support your specific goal at that time.

Be very careful not to draw on your own energy when working to heal something external. You can very quickly deplete yourself. Always make sure you center and ground, and monitor your own energy levels. You don't have to undertake a drastic working; sometimes slow, incremental work does more in the long run.

It's also important that you don't play god, either. You are not the know-all omniscient being. You can make a decision, but remember that you bear responsibility for that decision. You also know that everything is connected, so working to redress an imbalance in one area will most likely draw energy from elsewhere, which will likely cause an imbalance somewhere else. It's a closed system, with the entire world inside it.

Activism

For green witches, it's hard to look at what's happening in the world today and not feel anguish at how nature is crying out. Engaging in activity to redress the imbalances you feel in the world around you is balm for the wounded soul that despairs on the part of nature.

Activism is the process of working in the physical world to bring about social or other change, and it dovetails neatly with using your grimoire to support and inspire personal development through reflecting on your beliefs and values. Activism doesn't necessarily mean marching in demonstrations and engaging in protests. It means working to support an ethical practice, or to dissuade people or companies from acting unethically.

Reviewing your ethical reflections in Chapter 9 can help you pinpoint issues or subjects that you feel deserve your attention and support. What values are you passionate about? Where can you work to support those values? Review your grimoire as well. Is there a topic that you return to throughout your workings? Is there a way to pursue that topic and work toward it in the world at large?

Change begins at the local level. Support local shops and creators. Look into local artisans and independent businesses; read up on their missions and support those you agree with. Investigate co-ops; consumer cooperatives are autonomous collectives of people who buy and sell things in a jointly owned business, working for mutual benefit. Everyone contributes, and everyone gets something out of it.

Purchasing power is one of the most effective weapons you can wield. It sounds anticlimactic, because most of us think in terms of working against a large corporation whose ethical practices we don't support. A conglomerate won't miss your $5 purchase. But the independent business can benefit from that $5 much more; proportionally, the impact is larger. Think in terms of what your money can do in a different place. You may spend a few more dollars locally in an independent bookshop, but you're investing in people, not a corporation. It's not about how much money you pay; it's about the energy you move and the direction it moves in.

The idea that if something is easier it is automatically a better process is a sweeping generalization that innovation and commercialism have made over the past decades. Saving time can take us away from an experience that we might otherwise have learned from. As innovation advances, we step further and further away from working with our hands and being aware of where our materials come from. This isn't to say that innovation and saving time are bad things; I certainly appreciate not having to use a washboard and mangle to clean my clothes. I appreciate being able to plant a vegetable garden for enjoyment instead of survival. But distancing ourselves from the land and nature has had consequences, and one of those consequences is a widespread lack of understanding that humanity and the natural world are part of each other. This leads to disinterest and a lack of respect for nature that results in abuse, lack of engagement, and frustration on the part of people who can see the damage being done as a result. Activism won't fix these things, but it allows you expression of your personal power at the community level.

ACTIVISM EXHAUSTION

Exhausting yourself in the pursuit of redressing wrongs and fighting for causes you believe in is very common. No one can be perfect all the time. Do what you can when you can. Exhausting the opposition is a tactic used by forces throughout time. You can find yourself engaging with issues over and over, your energy being nibbled away by smaller things like arguments with people who aren't engaging with you in good faith.

There is no shame in stepping back for a bit. Picking your battles is also wise. You are working with so many other people fighting the good fight that if you sit down to recoup your energy and rejuvenate, you will not be missed. Don't feel guilty for taking a rest to recoup energy, either. You're no help to anyone if you wear yourself out. Then you're benched even longer than you would have been by taking a rest, and the repercussions may reach further than you expect.

Don't hesitate to use your journal as a place to pour out emotional responses, including anger, despair, and fear. Your grimoire can be a reassuring partner.

RITUAL TO RELEASE FEELINGS OF NOT DOING ALL YOU CAN

We always wish we could do more. But don't kick yourself because you can't make sweeping changes in whatever forum you're looking at. You are one person, and if all you had to do was work to shine light on one ethical issue, sure, you could devote all your time and energy to that. But you have a family to take care of; you have a home to run and maintain; you have friends; you have a job. Do what you can.

This ritual is designed to help you release guilt, anger, and negative feelings about yourself and your impact. Water is an element associated with emotion, flow, purification, and transformation, which is ideal for this ritual. Perform it outdoors somewhere where you can pour water on the ground.

WHAT YOU NEED
- Bowl of water (any material, any size)
- Your grimoire and a writing utensil

WHAT TO DO

1. Center and ground.

2. Hold the bowl of water in your hands. Close your eyes and allow the feelings of inadequacy, anger, frustration, and other negative emotions to flow out of you and into the water. The water can hold an infinite amount of feelings; don't hold back. You may find yourself dredging up older resentment and reactions while you do this; that's not unexpected. Let everything go.

3. If you like, you can talk the feelings out of you and give them to the water that way. Don't censor what you say; everything is valid during this ritual.

4. When you feel that you have exhausted the feelings, breathe deeply for a few cycles to rebalance, in case the uprising of emotion destabilized your centering. When you are steady again, hold the bowl of water up and say:

I release all that holds me back.
I release feelings of negativity.
I release energy that is not vibrating in harmony with my goal.
I release the sense of inadequacy that hampers my efforts.
I release frustration.

5. Tip the bowl and pour the water out, saying:

I honor my goals and my dreams.
I honor my commitment to a better world.

6. Journal your experience in your grimoire.

Developing Your Relationship with the World

It's very easy to settle into a comfortable routine as a witch. This is the way you've done it, so you continue to do it; it's calming and it flows well. What is comfortable, however, is not always the best way to grow. You need to step out of your comfort zone, even if it's just dipping a toe outside your tried-and-true routine. Reading about different practices and ideologies is a good way to stretch your mental muscles in pursuit of this goal.

Move out into the world and interact with the energy out there. This is good for at least two reasons: First, it stimulates your own energy and observation skills, and challenges your awareness. Second, it's good to stir local energy by interacting with it. It will help you keep in better touch with your area's energy and be able to notice when something changes.

TRAVEL

Travel can challenge your notion of nature, too, and it doesn't have to be to another country or continent. Day trips offer you the chance to sense energy in a different location and compare it to your home base.

If you do make a major trip, bring your grimoire along. As you interact with the energy at your destination, try to engage with each of your senses one by one. Describe your experiences in your grimoire. How do the energies of your travel destination differ from the ones at home? How are they similar? What do they remind you of? How would you use them in a spiritual or magical context? Don't forget bodies of water and spiritual or religious sites.

> Don't forget people are a facet of nature. You don't have to isolate yourself to interact with nature.

If you're traveling out of your country, take along a small journal to use as a travel grimoire. Record your experiences for reference and broadening your understanding and experience of the world. Consider it a supplement to your main grimoire. Remember, cuttings or pressed plant matter are usually illegal to bring across major country borders.

CURRENT EVENTS

Keep up on current events that impact your areas of ethical importance. This can be tricky, because you can be drawn in emotionally and it can spiral out of control. Curate your intake; focus on news about nature or cultural news if certain topics like politics become overwhelming.

Politics is an enormous part of what drives our world, impacts nature, and influences consumption. It's also one of the most devastating topics that can quickly lead to burnout if you immerse yourself deeply and repeatedly. Activism is often associated with politics, but if the national or global levels are too stressful for you, look to your local civic level instead. Change begins locally, remember. It's easier to work closer to home than on a sweeping national level, and it's rewarding to see things change for the better on a level that directly impacts your community.

Recommended References and Resources

IF YOU ARE INTERESTED IN PAPERCRAFT:

www.annespapercreations.com

IF YOU ARE INTERESTED IN FOUNTAIN OR DIP PENS
AND BOTTLED INK:

www.wonderpens.ca (Canada)
www.gouletpens.com (USA)
www.cultpens.com (UK)

IF YOU ARE INTERESTED IN BOOKBINDING,
CHECK OUT JENNIFER'S TERRIFIC TUTORIALS ON *YOUTUBE*:

www.youtube.com/user/SeaLemonDIY

Bibliography

Belfrage, Sue. *Down to the River and Up to the Trees: Discover the Magic of Forest Therapy and Many More Natural Wonders*. London: Thorsons, 2017.

Blackthorn, Amy. *Blackthorn's Botanical Magic: The Green Witch's Guide to Essential Oils for Spellcraft, Ritual & Healing*. Newburyport, MA: Weiser Books, 2018.

———. *Sacred Smoke: Clear Away Negative Energies and Purify Body, Mind, and Spirit*. Newburyport, MA: Weiser Books, 2019.

Cush, Denise, ed. *Celebrating Planet Earth, a Pagan/Christian Conversation: First Steps in Interfaith Dialogue*. Winchester, UK: Moon Books, 2015.

Danaan, Clea. *Voices of the Earth: The Path of Green Spirituality*. Woodbury, MN: Llewellyn Publications, 2009.

Dugan, Ellen. *Garden Witch's Herbal: Green Magick, Herbalism & Spirituality*. Woodbury, MN: Llewellyn Publications, 2009.

Gourlay, Susie. "Unraveled Oracle." *Knit Natural*. Accessed January 4, 2020. www.knitnatural.com/unraveled.html.

Greer, John Michael. *The Druid Magic Handbook: Ritual Magic Rooted in the Living Earth*. San Francisco: Red Wheel/Weiser, 2007.

Haskell, David George. *The Songs of Trees: Stories from Nature's Great Connectors*. New York: Viking, 2017.

Ivens, Sarah. *Forest Therapy: Seasonal Ways to Embrace Nature for a Happier You*. New York: Da Capo Press, 2018.

Kimmerer, Robin Wall. *Braiding Sweetgrass: Indigenous Wisdom, Scientific Knowledge, and the Teachings of Plants*. Minneapolis, MN: Milkweed Editions, 2013.

Kort, Barry. "Foundations of Ethics: Contribution of Lawrence Kohlberg, Carol Gilligan, John Rawls, Lonnie Athens, James Gilligan, Suzanne Retzinger, René Girard, Jean Jacques Rousseau, Thomas Hobbes, and John Locke." Accessed January 6, 2020. https://barrykort.wordpress.com/article/foundations-of-ethics-3iyoslgwsp412-10/.

Murphy-Hiscock, Arin. *The Green Witch: Your Complete Guide to the Natural Magic of Herbs, Flowers, Essential Oils, and More.* Avon, MA: Adams Media, 2017.

———. *The House Witch: Your Complete Guide to Creating a Magical Space with Rituals and Spells for Hearth and Home.* Avon, MA: Adams Media, 2018.

———. *Protection Spells: Clear Negative Energy, Banish Unhealthy Influences, and Embrace Your Power.* Avon, MA: Adams Media, 2018.

———. *Spellcrafting: Strengthen the Power of Your Craft by Creating and Casting Your Own Unique Spells.* Avon, MA: Adams Media, 2020.

Nock, Judy Ann. *The Modern Witchcraft Guide to Magickal Herbs: Your Complete Guide to the Hidden Powers of Herbs.* Avon, MA: Adams Media, 2019.

———. *A Witch's Grimoire: Create Your Own Book of Shadows.* Avon, MA: Adams Media, 2005.

Toll, Maia. *The Illustrated Herbiary: Guidance and Rituals from 36 Bewitching Botanicals.* North Adams, MA: Storey Publishing, 2018.

Zakroff, Laura Tempest. *Weave the Liminal: Living Modern Traditional Witchcraft.* Woodbury, MN: Llewellyn Publications, 2019.

The Magical Associations of Natural Items

NO GRIMOIRE WOULD BE COMPLETE WITHOUT reference lists of correspondences and natural energies. Remember that while traditional associations or associations observed by others are a place to start and can be important pieces of information that can contribute to your information, they shouldn't be the sum of it. It's important that you do your own research and exploration, interacting with as many different materials and ingredients as possible to make your own direct observations to write down in your reference section of your grimoire.

The following lists of magical associations, like the other lists in this book, have been assembled over my years of practice and include both my own associations as well as traditional correspondences. Apart from personal experimentation and work, my sources over the years have included such books as Mrs. M. Grieve's *A Modern Herbal*, Scott Cunningham's *Encyclopedia of Magical Herbs*, Paul Beyerl's *The Master Book of Herbalism* and *A Compendium of Herbal Magick*, and Jamie Wood's *The Wicca Herbal: Recipes, Magick, and Abundance*.

Herbs and Plants

ALLSPICE
prosperity, luck, healing, purification, protection, money

ALMOND
love, money, healing, wisdom

ANGELICA
protection, hex breaker, healing, psychic abilities, house blessing, purification

ANISE
psychic abilities, lust, luck, purification, love

APPLE
love, healing, peace

ASH
protection, strength, healing, prosperity

BASIL
love, trust, abundance, prosperity, courage, discipline, protection, marriage, purification, luck, mental abilities

BAY
protection, purification, endurance, fidelity, psychic powers, divination, wisdom, strength

BAYBERRY
abundance, prosperity

BENZOIN
purification, healing, prosperity

BIRCH
protection, purification, new beginnings, children

CARNATION
protection, strength, energy, luck, healing

CATNIP
cats, love, beauty, happiness, tranquility, luck

CEDAR
healing, purification, protection, prosperity

CHAMOMILE
purification, healing, soothes anxiety, gently heals bad luck, soothes children

CHICKWEED
animals, love, fidelity, healing, weight loss

CINNAMON
healing, love, lust, success, purification, protection, money, psychic awareness

CINQUEFOIL (FIVE-FINGER GRASS)
eloquence, cunning, money, protection, sleep, prophetic dreams, purification, love

CLOVE
protection, mental abilities, attraction, purification, comfort

CLOVER
lust, hex breaking, prosperity, purification, love, luck, protection, success, fidelity, comfort

COMFREY (BONESET)
healing, prosperity, protection, travel

CORIANDER
healing, love, lust

CUMIN
protection, anti-theft, love, fidelity

CYPRESS
protection, comfort, healing

DAFFODIL
luck, fertility, love

DAISY
nature spirits, love, hope, children

DANDELION
longevity, intuition, spiritual and emotional cleanser, enhances psychic ability

DILL
protection, love, attraction, money, strength, luck, mental abilities, weight loss, eases sleep

ECHINACEA
healing

ELDER, ELDERFLOWER
beauty, divination, prosperity, purification, house blessing, healing, sleep, protection from lightning

ELM
love, protection

EUCALYPTUS
protection, healing

EYEBRIGHT
truth, certainty, psychic ability, pierces through illusion

FENNEL
courage, strength, cleansing

FERN
invisibility, love, chastity, protection, unlocking doors

FEVERFEW
love, fidelity, protection, healing

FLAX
money, protection, beauty, healing

GARDENIA
love, attraction, harmony, healing, peace, meditation

GARLIC
healing, house blessing, protection, lust, anti-theft

GERANIUM
love, healing, courage, protection, fertility

GINGER
healing, love, money, energy

GRASS
serenity, adaptability

HAWTHORN
protection, fertility, happiness

HAZEL
mental abilities, fertility, protection, wisdom, luck

HEATHER
protection, rain, luck

HELIOTROPE
clairvoyance, psychic abilities, health, money

HIBISCUS
love, lust, divination, harmony, peace

HONEYSUCKLE
abundance, luck, prosperity, eases sorrow, enhances psychic abilities
(do not use the berries; they are poisonous)

HOPS
healing, sleep

HYACINTH
love, comfort, happiness, protection

HYSSOP
purification, protection

IRIS
purification, blessing, wisdom, faith, valor

JASMINE
love, attraction, prosperity, tranquility, meditation, spirituality, harmony

JUNIPER
cleansing, purification, protection against accidents, love, anti-theft, fertility, psychic abilities, protection against illness

LAVENDER
healing, love, happiness, sleep, tranquility, protection, purification, peace, house blessing, wisdom, children, marriage, heals grief and guilt

LEMON
purification, love, protection, happiness

LICORICE
love, lust, protection, fidelity

LILAC
protection, beauty, love, psychic abilities, purification, prosperity, banishing negative energy

LILY
protection, love antidote, truth, elimination of hexes, rebirth and cycles

LILY OF THE VALLEY
concentration and mental ability, happiness

LIME
love, purification, luck, sleep

LOTUS
blessing, meditation, protection, spirituality

MAPLE
sweetness, prosperity, marriage, love, money

MARIGOLD
positive energy, protective, peace, eases legal stress, increases psychic awareness

MARJORAM
protection, love, happiness, health, money, marriage, comfort

MEADOWSWEET
peace, love, happiness, psychic awareness

MINT
purification, health, love, success, clarity of mind, protects travelers, attracts money, preserves health

MISTLETOE
healing, protection, love, fertility, sleep, luck

MOSS
perseverance, patience, nurturing, grounding, serenity, calm

MUGWORT
divination, protection, healing, strength, lust, psychic power, fertility, protects travelers

NETTLE
cleansing, protects from danger, protects health

NUTMEG
clairvoyance, health, luck, fidelity

OAK
purification, protection, prosperity, health and healing, money, fertility, luck, strength

ONION
healing, protection, purification

ORANGE
love, joy, purification, prosperity

OREGANO
peace

PANSY
divination, communication, happiness, love

PARSLEY
healing, lust, fertility, love, passion, protection, hex breaker, prosperity, purification, protection, eases grief

PATCHOULI
money, fertility, lust, clairvoyance, divination, love, attraction

PEPPER
protection, purification

PINE
prosperity, healing, purification, fertility

POPPY
fertility, abundance, sleep, love, tranquility, prosperity

ROSE
healing, love, conciliation, harmony, protection, restoration, self-love, attracts love and good fortune, heals trouble, enhances psychic ability

ROSEMARY
cleansing, protection, healing, longevity, improves memory and concentration

ROWAN (MOUNTAIN ASH)
purification, house blessing, protection, healing, psychic abilities, wisdom, strengthens spells

RUE
protection, mental abilities, purification, health, comfort

SAGE
healing, longevity, good health, psychic awareness, protection

SNAPDRAGON
protection from illusion or deception, reflects negative energy

ST. JOHN'S WORT
courage, power of the sun, fertility, purification, healing, positive energy

SUNFLOWER
happiness, success, health, fertility, hospitality, family

TARRAGON
cleansing, regeneration, transformation

THYME
purification, psychic cleansing, courage, divination, healing, enhances memory, eases sleep

TULIP
prosperity, abundance, protection, love, happiness

VALERIAN (ALL-HEAL)
purification, protection, healing, love, sleep, attraction

VANILLA
love, prosperity, lust, energy, mental abilities, creativity

VERBENA (VERVAIN)
purification, protection, blessings, success, communication with nature spirits

VIOLET
tranquility, love, luck, protection, healing, peace, hope, harmony

WALNUT
healing, mental abilities

WILLOW
communication, eloquence, protection, healing, love, dreams

YARROW
marriage, courage, love and friendship, healing, psychic abilities, hex breaking

Magical Associations of Fruit

APPLE
health, longevity, love

BANANA
fertility, strength

BLACKBERRY
prosperity, protection, abundance

BLUEBERRY
tranquility, peace, protection, prosperity

CRANBERRY
protection, healing

GRAPE
prosperity, fertility

KIWI
fertility, love

LEMON
purification, protection, health

LIME
happiness, purification, healing

MANGO
spirituality, happiness

ORANGE
joy, health, purification

PEACH
spirituality, fertility, love, harmony

PEAR
health, prosperity, love

PINEAPPLE
prosperity, luck, protection

PLUM
love, tranquility

RASPBERRY
strength, courage, healing

STRAWBERRY
love, peace, happiness, luck

Trees

APPLE
life, longevity, fertility, love, healing

ASH
strength, intellect, willpower, protection, justice, balance and harmony, skill, travel, weather, wisdom

BIRCH
cleansing, protection, purification, children

CEDAR
healing, spirituality, purification, protection, prosperity, harmony

ELDER
protection (especially against being struck by lightning), prosperity, healing

HAWTHORN
fertility, harmony, happiness, the otherworld, protection

HAZEL
luck, fertility, protection, wishes

HONEYSUCKLE
psychic awareness, harmony, healing, prosperity, happiness

MAPLE
love, prosperity, health, abundance

OAK
defense, thunder, strength, courage, healing, longevity, strength, protection, good fortune

PINE
cleansing, purification, healing, clarity of mind, prosperity, protection

POPLAR
prosperity, communication, exorcism, purification

ROWAN
psychic ability, divination, healing, protection, peace, creativity, success, change and transformation

WILLOW
growth, renewal, love, tranquility, harmony, protection, healing

WITCH HAZEL
protection, healing, peace

YEW
death, spirits, the otherworld

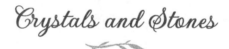

Crystals and Stones

AMETHYST
psychic power, truth, balance, protection, healing

AVENTURINE
luck, prosperity, health

BLOODSTONE
health (especially of the blood), protection

CARNELIAN
success, manifestation

CITRINE
calms nightmares, aids in digestion, focuses the mind, enhances creativity

HEMATITE
defense, healing, justice, grounding excess or unbalanced energy, deflects negativity

JADE
wisdom, prosperity, fertility, health, protection

JASPER
grounding, stabilizing energy, protection, courage

LAPIS LAZULI
leadership, communication, stress relief, creativity, joy, harmony

MALACHITE
fertility, earth mysteries, connection to nature

MOONSTONE
protection during travel, children, love, peace

MOSS AGATE
healing, calm, stress relief

OBSIDIAN (BLACK AND SNOWFLAKE)
protection

QUARTZ, CLEAR
amplifies energy, stores power, enhances psychic ability, absorbs negativity

QUARTZ, ROSE
self-esteem, self-love, emotional healing, affection, transforms negative energy into positive

QUARTZ, SMOKY
grounding, clears obstacles, strengthens intuition, helps thoughts turn to action and goals to reality

SODALITE
wisdom, balancing emotions

TIGER'S-EYE
strength, courage, luck, prosperity

TURQUOISE
protects, gentle strength, focuses the mind and will

Colors

BLACK
protection, fertility, mystery

BROWN
stability, home, career

DARK BLUE
healing, justice

DARK GREEN
prosperity, money, nature

GOLD
health, prosperity, solar energy, masculine energy

GRAY
calm, spirit work, gentle closure, neutralizing energy or situations

LIGHT BLUE
truth, spirituality, tranquility, peace

LIGHT GREEN
healing, wishes

ORANGE
success, speed, career, action

PINK
affection, friendship

PURPLE
occult power, spirituality

RED
life, passion, action, energy

SILVER
purity, divination, psychic work, feminine energy, spirit, lunar energy

VIOLET
mysticism, meditation, spirituality

WHITE
purity, psychic development

YELLOW
intellectual matters, communication

Index

D

Death, honoring, 180, 190–93
Decorations, 55–56
Dedication ritual, 62–63
Deities, thanking, 154–56
Deities, working with, 22, 63,
    79, 127
Design ideas, 15–107
Digital grimoire, 39–42, 58, 99.
    See also Grimoires
Divinations
    candles and, 129
    crystal ball and, 128
    daily life and, 129–30
    dowsing rod and, 128
    energy and, 126
    evaluating, 67
    explanation of, 126–27
    grimoire and, 126–38
    intuition and, 126–31, 139,
        148–49, 194, 196
    methods of, 127–29
    mirrors and, 128
    omens and, 129–30
    oracle decks and, 127–28
    overview of, 127–29
    pendulum and, 128
    record of, 23, 66–67, 111,
        130–38
    reviewing, 133
    scrying and, 128–29
    speculum and, 128–29
    spellwork and, 126–31
    stones and, 127, 128
    subconscious and, 126–33
    tarot decks and, 127–28
    templates for, 134–38
    water and, 128
Dowsing rod, 128
Dreams

collection of, 110, 161
journaling about, 166
record of, 23, 41, 54, 68
subconscious and, 166
symbolism of, 166

E

Earth element, 77
Einstein, Albert, 128
Elements
    air, 78
    earth, 77
    energy of, 77–78, 81, 113–14
    fire, 78–79, 84
    water, 79–80, 128
Emotions, releasing, 28, 68,
    162–64, 212–14
Energy
    absorbing, 13–14, 112
    communication with, 126
    death and, 191–93
    divinations and, 126
    of elements, 77–78, 81,
        113–14
    energy work, 12, 14, 113,
        125–59, 193–94
    flow of, 196–97, 201–2
    healing energy, 73, 139,
        194–95, 208–9
    journaling and, 163–64
    lunar energy, 72–74, 172
    of materials, 204–7
    of nature, 16
    of plants, 85–87, 97–106,
        118–24, 205–6
    raising, 194–95
    releasing, 118–22, 163–64,
        191–93, 208–9, 212–14
    seasonal energies, 76–77, 172
    sensing, 113–16

Herbs. *See also* Plants
  art activities with, 102–7
  associations of, 228–35
  for blessing charm, 60–61
  for blessing wand, 119–22
  charging, 123–24
  citing references on, 96
  collecting, 88, 97–99
  describing, 86–89, 93
  gardens for, 119
  geographic information on,
    87, 94
  illustrating, 87, 93
  magic of, 86–89, 95
  medical information on,
    87, 94
  for paper making, 45–47
  pressing, 88, 100–103
  record of, 86–95
  for sacred space, 118–24
  samples of, 97–99
  for smoke cleansing,
    118–19, 207
  strewing, 123
  templates for, 90–95
  toxicity of, 87, 94
  uses of, 87–88, 94
  warnings about, 87, 89, 94
Hoodoo, 118

I

Ideas, brainstorming, 28,
  30–32
Ideas, finding, 15–107
Illustrations, drawing,
  55–56, 87
Incense, 59, 72, 118
Index, creating, 36, 69–71, 96
Information
  citing, 24–25, 71, 96, 157

  including in grimoire, 18–42,
    65–96, 110–216
  organizing, 41–43, 65, 68–69,
    157–59
  taking notes on, 26, 30–31,
    157–59
Inks, 49–54, 219. *See also* Pens
Inspiration
  from brainstorming, 28, 30–31
  from deities, 22
  for green witch, 22–24,
    28–31, 42, 59, 67
  from grimoires, 59
  record of, 67
Interactions
  with grimoire, 125–59, 227
  with materials, 127–28, 227
  with nature, 165, 216
  with world, 11–12, 24, 192,
    196–97, 215–16
Intuition
  divinations and, 126–31, 139,
    148–49, 194, 196
  note-taking for, 158
  for spellcraft, 126–31, 139,
    148–49, 194, 196

J

Journals
  apps for, 40–41, 167
  art journals, 56, 67
  benefits of, 13–14, 161–63
  grimoire as, 11–14, 18–19,
    161–72
  ideas for, 165–67, 171–72,
    183–84, 201, 208,
    213–14
  insight from, 13–14, 26–27,
    162–65, 170–71
  of learning, 11–14, 26–28

N

Natural disasters, 193–95
Natural items, associations of, 225–40
Natural phenomena, 22, 129–30
Nature
    activism and, 197, 210–12
    clergy for, 195
    cycle of, 83, 173, 190–93
    energy of, 16
    environment and, 196–97, 202–7
    interacting with, 165, 216
    leaf prints, 102–3
    nature art activities, 102–7
    needs of, 194–95
    rhythms of, 173, 192
    spirits of, 22, 62, 79, 118, 194–96
    stamping activity, 106–7
    walks in, 165
Note-taking, 26, 30–31, 157–59

O

Oil lamps, 83–84
Omens, interpreting, 129–30
Oracle decks, 127–28
Organization tips, 41–43, 65, 68–69, 157–59
Orthogonal axis, 178, 179, 180
Outreach, importance of, 197

P

Paper
    choosing, 44–45
    color of, 48–49, 54
    gluing, 31–32, 35–36, 44, 55, 58
    inks and, 49–54
    making, 45–47
    natural materials for, 45, 48–49
    pens and, 49–54
    resources for, 219
    types of, 44–49
    weight of, 44
Pendulum, 128
Pens
    dip pens, 50
    fountain pens, 49–50
    inks for, 49–54
    quill pens, 51–53
    resources for, 219
Pentacle, 81
Philosophy, 11–12, 17, 28
Photographs, 30, 32, 41, 55–56, 67, 98–99
Planets, 22
Plants
    art activities with, 102–7
    associations of, 228–35
    citing references on, 96
    collecting, 88, 97–99, 104–5
    describing, 86–89, 93
    energy of, 85–87, 97–106, 118–24, 205–6
    gardens for, 83, 119, 211
    geographic information on, 87, 94
    illustrating, 87, 93
    magic of, 85–107
    medical information on, 87, 94
    pressing, 88, 100–103
    record of, 85–107
    for sacred space, 118–24
    samples of, 97–99
    for smoke cleansing, 118–19, 207
    templates for, 90–95
    toxicity of, 87, 94

Transformations, 192, 199–200, 213–14
Travel, 89, 168, 215–16
Traveler's Notebooks, 36–37
Tree associations, 237–38
Trees, record of, 86–88. *See also* Plants

V

Values, 63, 173–89, 210. *See also* Morals
Vegetable gardens, 83, 119, 211
Vegetable stamp activity, 106–7
Vision boards, 30, 41

W

Wands, making, 119–22
Wands, using, 81, 83
Water, blessing, 80, 123–24
Water element, 79–80, 82, 128
Wildcrafting, 69, 97, 165
Wisdom, honoring, 188–89
Witchcraft practice
    divinations for, 126–33
    ethical practices, 21–22, 110, 173–89, 210–16
    for honoring death, 180, 190–93
    record of, 11–14, 21–28, 67–68, 81–107, 110–59, 161–72, 199–216
    sacred space for, 17, 80–81, 117–24
    spellwork and, 139–46
    spiritual practice, 12–14, 28, 80–85, 116–17, 174–76, 184–93, 207
    techniques for, 113–22, 213–14
Witnessing, 189–93, 199–200

World
    activism and, 197, 210–12, 216
    behavior toward, 196–97
    current events in, 216
    everyday world, 196–97
    interaction with, 11–12, 24, 192, 196–97, 215–16
    politics in, 216
    travel in, 215–16

"The Green Witch *is a delightful guide to nature magic. It's filled with practical recipes for herbal blends and potions, the properties of essential oils, and lots of ideas for healing and relaxation.*"
—BUSTLE

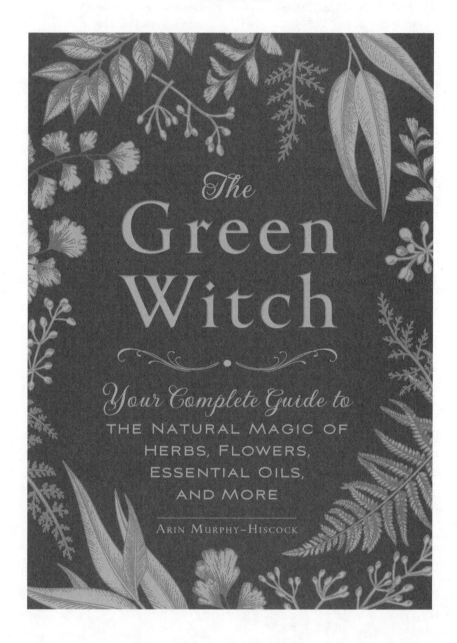

PICK UP OR DOWNLOAD YOUR COPY TODAY!